HAPPINESS * SUCCESS * ROMANCE
GOOD FORTUNE

Use Your Sun Signs to Realize Your Dreams *in 1988!*

Whatever you desire can be yours if you look to the stars for guidance. Sydney Omarr, America's foremost astrologer, will put you in the driver's seat and show you how to direct your energies toward happiness and success—no matter what your goals.

A brand-new year of exciting possibilities awaits you. Read about how the sun and the moon reveal the outer and inner you; track your planets of fate, fortune, and power; be the best you can be, using your sun sign fashion and beauty tips.

Be surprised and delighted as each of your dreams comes to life. Follow the wisdom of your sun sign and get ready for a wonderful 1988!

15 MONTHS OF DAILY PREDICTIONS

1·9·8·8

SCORPIO

(OCTOBER 23—NOVEMBER 21)

SYDNEY OMARR'S

DAY-BY-DAY ASTROLOGICAL GUIDE

A SIGNET BOOK

NEW AMERICAN LIBRARY

NAL BOOKS ARE AVAILABLE AT QUANTITY DISCOUNTS
WHEN USED TO PROMOTE PRODUCTS OR SERVICES.
FOR INFORMATION PLEASE WRITE TO PREMIUM MARKETING DIVISION.
NEW AMERICAN LIBRARY. 1633 BROADWAY.
NEW YORK. NEW YORK 10019.

Copyright © 1987 by Sydney Omarr

Sydney Omarr is syndicated worldwide by Los Angeles Times Syndicate.

SIGNET TRADEMARK REG. U.S. PAT. OFF. AND FOREIGN COUNTRIES
REGISTERED TRADEMARK—MARCA REGISTRADA
HECHO EN CHICAGO, U.S.A.

SIGNET, SIGNET CLASSIC, MENTOR, ONYX, PLUME, MERIDIAN AND
NAL BOOKS are published by NAL PENGUIN INC.,
1633 Broadway, New York, New York 10019

First Printing, July, 1987

1 2 3 4 5 6 7 8 9

PRINTED IN THE UNITED STATES OF AMERICA

CONTENTS

Introduction

You and the Universe in 1988

What's written in the stars for you in 1988? Like millions of Americans who turn to astrology for fun, curiosity or guidance, you're in for a fascinating experience as you explore the cosmos in this unique way. Unlike other arts or sciences, astrology can give you specific details on who you are and where you're going and immediate practical advice on how to deal with the whole range of problems and situations that crop up in daily life. It's no wonder that the lure of discovering a real human connection with the universe has kept people in all walks of life, from tycoons to the man on the street, intrigued with astrology.

As you discover astrology for yourself, you'll learn that, far from being a vague, intuitive art shrouded in mystery, it is quite a precise language that communicates in a very orderly and specific way. Yet it retains a sense of wonder and mystery. We marvel how those faraway planets can tell us so much about ourselves— with such uncanny accuracy! Yet, haven't there been times when you've felt an unexplained "pull" in a certain direction, or times when everything seems to be going haywire, times when nobody seems to understand you and other times when you seem to have hit a lucky roll? Astrology offers explanations to these baffling conditions, points out trends and cycles and suggests solutions to difficulties or alternate courses to take. It brings the happenings in the universe down to human terms, though it never dictates a moral code or involves the worship of deities.

Though it is a precise and demanding study, no one can deny that there is a mysterious spiritual quality about astrology. And because it is often used for prediction, it has been the subject of much misunderstanding through the ages, especially when fortune tellers and unscrupulous practitioners masqueraded under its banner. Today, astrology has become recognized as a respectable endeavor practiced by qualified professionals who don't gaze into crystal balls, tell fortunes or operate out of gypsy caravans. Most of the 10,000 or more astrologers in the United States are serious consultants accredited by one of several reputable astrological associations.

Working with precise scientific calculations, often done by computer, today's professional astrologer adds interpretive insight that goes beyond the scientific dimension. This requires great skill, knowledge of human behavior and relationships as well as planetary happenings, which is why leaders of government and corporations, bankers and dictators often consider astrological conditions before making major decisions.

When forecasts and predictions are involved, some inevitable questions arise, such as: Where do *I* fit in? How much free will do I have? Can I do anything about an unfavorable forecast? Or, on a supposedly critical day, why did everything go smoothly?

The responsible astrologer will answer: *You* make the difference and the decisions. Astrology can point the direction, give you clues about the kind of energy prevailing on a specific day, put events in a grand perspective, so they seem easier to handle. But what you do with this knowledge is up to you.

Can you study and use astrology on your own? Why not? This book will give you basic tools for taking your own "star trek" through the zodiac. You'll be amazed how even a basic knowledge of astrology gives you valuable insights about others. Your most important tool is your own horoscope, a map of the heavens based on the happenings at the moment you were born. This tells you about your potential in every area of life, what talents to develop, where to look for a profitable career, even what kind of partner to choose for business and love. It can target your trouble spots in relationships—give you clues about why you have difficulty communicating with someone and how to improve the situation. It can help you improve the quality of your life by giving you hints about health and how to make the most of your strengths to protect yourself from stress, to make the most of your physical appearance.

Then there is the matter of timing. Astrology helps you pick the perfect moment to initiate a plan, sign a contract, go to a party, meet someone special or close a deal. It's all based on an understanding of the way the energies of the planets are acting and interacting at a given time. This book will explain what forces are harmonizing or conflicting. It reveals which planet affects your communications for better or worse and what the '88 outlook will be. You'll learn which phase of the moon is best for starting new ventures, and when to expect a major transition in your life.

We'll start with the groundwork of astrology. You'll learn to speak its language and discover what those baffling signs and symbols really mean.

Then we'll explore the horoscope—how each planetary force affects you and the events in your life. The fun part comes next: what you really want to know about picking a partner, your chances for being rich and famous by playing up the strengths of your sign and playing down its weaknesses. We'll even show you how to set up a success timetable for '88 to benefit from positive planetary influences.

For your day-to-day living, there are fifteen months of personal predictions. Each day there are highlights of the planetary, lunar and numerical cycles as they relate to your sign with custom-blended interpretations. What's more, you'll find the daily moon sign and lucky numbers for significant days.

So, whether you are new to astrology or a regular reader, let this guide put *you* in the universe in 1988. May the stars light your way to the happiest, healthiest year ever!

1

Astro-Lore

Did you know that . . .

- The signing of the Declaration of Independence may
  have been astrologically timed? Thomas Jefferson was
  an adept amateur astrologer who signed the document at 2 a.m, July 4, 1776, when the new nation
  would be born at a favorable moment.

- Astrology was a major influence in World War II?
  Adolf Hitler consulted several astrologers indepen-
  dently and based his decisions on a consensus of their
  opinions.

- The founder of analytic psychology, Carl Gustav Jung
  cast horoscopes of his patients and used them as diag-
  nostic aids?

- Hippocrates (460–377 B.C.), the "father of medicine,"
  said: "He who does not understand astrology is not a
  doctor but a fool"? The great Greek physician required that all his students have a knowledge of the
  stars.

- Astrology is for anglers hooked on fishing? Time
  your line for the last quarter or the new moon, when

11

the moon is in a water sign (Cancer, Scorpio or Pisces), for the best catch.

Financial wizard J. P. Morgan was such a devoted student of astrologer Evangeline Adams that he sent his top lawyer to defend her when she was involved in astrology's greatest public trial?

The legendary tenor Enrico Caruso never crossed the Atlantic until astrologer Evangeline Adams had approved the date?

Many kings and world leaders have ruled with the help of astrology? Queen Elizabeth I of England consulted astrologer John Dee. While Queen of France, Catherine de Medici relied on Nostradamus. In Bohemia, Rudolph II relied on two astrologer/astronomers Tycho Brahe and Johannes Kepler. In modern times, Winston Churchill employed astrologer Louis de Wohl to second-guess German maneuvers.

Napoleon had his horoscope cast, but is said to have ignored the advice of his astrologer before the battle of Waterloo?

The oldest recorded astrology is that of the Chinese, which is at least 5,000 years old?

The Chaldeans of ancient Mesopotamia were the fathers of modern-day astrology? Three thousand years ago, they divided the sky into twelve sections and distinguished between planets, which they called "wanderers" and fixed stars. Later, they endowed the planets with personalities, naming them after their gods. The elusive Mercury, which stays close to the sun, was named Nabu, the trickster. Venus became associated with Ishtar, goddess of love and fertility. Even then, the red planet Mars was named after the god of war, Nerval. Saturn was the stern avenger, Ninurta, and Jupiter was Marduk, king of the gods. Later the Greeks and Romans substituted the names of their own deities with corresponding personalities.

- The Roman Emperor Augustus minted coins bearing his sign symbol?

2

Star-Tracking:
The Groundwork of Astrology

Studying astrology is like putting together pieces of a puzzle to get an overview of a person or an event. We are actually composing a planetary portrait of a *moment in time* using many different elements which interact, adding color and shades of meaning to the picture.

The word "astrology," coming from the Greek words "astron" for star and "logos" for discourse, reveals that this study will be concerned with much more than just the placement of planets on a map of the heavens. It is involved with interpretation, making a commentary on how these distant bodies relate to each other and to our lives here on earth.

Ancient astronomers (astrology and astronomy were once the same) noted that certain heavenly bodies always moved on a pathway passing by the same fixed stars. These were called planets, derived from the word meaning "wanderer." Many of the stationary stars could be grouped together in constellations and imagined in the outline of animal shapes. So the route of the planets became known as the zodiac or "circle of animals" by the early Greeks (even though some objects and people connected with myths and legends were included).

Note that, in astrology, we only deal with the constellations that occur in the zodiac. Unlike astronomers, we are not concerned with happenings in the Big Dipper or Orion or Andromeda. Nor do we worry about supernovas, "black holes," other galaxies and celestial phenomena. However, the discovery of a new and distant planet moving along the zodiac pathway would cause great excitement.

The zodiac was originally divided into 12 equal 30-degree segments, each marked by a constellation which served as a sign post. As thousands of years passed, and the earth's axis changed, the constellations have actually "moved" from their original positions. But the twelve divisions or "signs" remain in the same place, still identified by their original symbols and meanings.

When astrologers observed that the movement of each planet through each sign seemed to coincide with a specific kind of event here on earth, they began to draw a composite picture of each 30-degree segment based on criteria they already used to define human behavior. These were the four *elements* found in nature (fire, earth, air and water), the *qualities* or how the sign operates (cardinal or activist, fixed or stable and mutable adaptable) and the *polarity* (masculine or feminine). Each sign was assigned one of each of the three variables—element, quality and polarity—beginning with Aries, which ushers in the spring equinox, and alternating in sequence around the zodiac. So no two signs have exactly the same mixture of ingredients. And, because the ingredients alternate around the zodiac, no sign is similar to the sign preceding it; in fact most signs seem to have opposite characteristics from their predecessors. For instance, active, energetic Aries is followed by slow-moving, stubborn Taurus. Sensitive, self-protective Cancer is followed by outgoing, confident Leo.

It's important to realize that the personality of a sign

was not endowed by chance, by myths or whim. Instead, it evolved systematically from the nature of these three variables (element, quality and polarity) as they alternate and progress around the zodiac. In the following rundown, you'll see how the ingredients combine to give each sign its special flavor.

Defining the Signs—By Element, Quality and Polarity

The Elements Are the Basic Character of the Sign

Ancients believed that everything was composed of mixtures of four elements: earth, air, fire and water. So it followed that the experience of a sign was also related to the elements. Since fire spreads energy, it was chosen to start the zodiac with Aries. Earth, which stands for the material world, followed. The mental world was symbolized by the element of air and the emotions by water. The same order was repeated through all twelve signs:

Fire—Aries
Earth—Taurus
Air—Gemini
Water—Cancer
Fire—Leo
Earth—Virgo
Air—Libra
Water—Scorpio
Fire—Sagittarius
Earth—Capricorn
Air—Aquarius
Water—Pisces

The *fire* signs (Aries, Leo and Sagittarius) show the

character of their element. They are dynamic, aggressive, passionate, daring. When the sun or any of the nine planets is passing through fire signs, they manifest fire sign characteristics. Each sign has a ruling celestial body, and the fire signs, naturally, have those that are especially bright. Red Mars rules Aries, the great sun rules Leo, and the huge glowing Jupiter rules Sagittarius.

The *earth* signs (Taurus, Virgo, Capricorn) symbolize the material world. They are the practical signs that make things happen, that look at life in a realistic way. Solidity, sustenance, continuity, building power are all the territory of the earth element. Their ruling planets reflect earth-sign concerns: Venus, the planet of physical beauty, rules Taurus; Mercury, planet of day-to-day communications rules Virgo, and Saturn, planet of duty, rules Capricorn.

The *air* signs (Gemini, Libra, Aquarius) reflect concerns of the mind: judgment, communications, ideal beauty, the intellect, ideas and concepts. The use of words to charm, discuss, debate and inspire is the province of their element. As ruler of Gemini, Mercury shows its mental, verbal side. Venus, ruler of Libra, is here concerned with ideals and justice. Uranus, ruler of Aquarius, bestows originality and inventiveness.

The *water* signs (Cancer, Pisces, Scorpio) manifest the element of emotions and intuition. Creativity in all its forms, nonverbal communication, sensitivity, mysticism, deep feelings and a fascination with mysteries are characteristics of this element and the signs it rules. The moon, which governs tides and strong feelings, rules the sign of Cancer; the distant mysterious Pluto rules Scorpio (along with Mars) and dreamy Neptune rules Pisces.

The Quality Is How the Sign Works
The signs work on three levels: action, stability and change. The cardinal or active signs are the initiators,

the signs who start things rolling. Aries, the first cardinal sign, heralds the coming of spring. Cancer happens at the onset of summer, Libra ushers in fall and Capricorn initiates winter.

The fixed signs come at the height of the season, during periods of growth, when stability is needed. Taurus comes during the blossoming of spring, Leo during the full bloom of summer, Scorpio during the harvest of fall, and Aquarius in the height of winter. These are the periods when things are accomplished.

The mutable signs bring on the change of seasons. These are the flexible signs, that change and adjust easily. Gemini is sparkling, witty, a gadabout which takes spring into summer. Virgo, practical and analytical, takes summer into the busy harvest season. Sagittarius, another energetic sign, moves fall into winter; then Pisces, emotional and romantic, prepares for the birth of spring. "Change," "versatility" and "adaptability" are key words for the mutable signs.

Male or Female, Yin or Yang: Each Sign Has a Polarity

The signs of the zodiac are also grouped by polarities which are valuable indicators of the way energies balance out at a given time. Each sign is either *positive* (male, active and "Yang") or *negative* (female, passive and "Yin"). If too many planets at a given moment are located in positive polarities, there might be too much aggressive action, and a great need to stop and reflect. If the scales tip toward the female negative polarities, then more get-up-and-go may be needed. Aries starts the zodiac as a positive sign, Taurus then follows as negative and so the polarities alternate through the zodiac. As the lots are cast, the end result is that all air and fire signs are masculine, all earth and water are feminine.

Masculine, active, positive, Yang signs:
Aries, Gemini, Leo, Libra, Sagittarius, Aquarius

Female, passive, negative, Yin signs:
Taurus, Cancer, Virgo, Scorpio, Capricorn, Pisces

Putting the Pieces Together for the Overall Picture

Aries: March 21–April 19
The Pieces: Fire element, cardinal quality, masculine polarity.

The Picture: First in the zodiac, Aries epitomizes all the dynamic energy need to emerge in the physical world. Aries announces its presence with the motto: "I am." It is pioneering, daring, a positive thinker. It is also very self-centered like a newborn child. It is a doer—an actor, not a reactor.

Taurus: April 20–May 20
The Pieces: Earth element, fixed quality, feminine polarity.

The Picture: The motto of Taurus, "I have," sums up this security-minded earth sign. Spring is also the season of growing and materializing in nature so it follows that those of Taurus's influence like to be close to nature, surrounded by green, growing things. The sign is stable, patient, with the great endurance and stubborness of a fixed sign. Taurus's negative polarity makes it receptive, reactive, a lover of comfort and ease.

Gemini: May 21–June 21
The Pieces: Air element, mutable quality, masculine polarity.

The Picture: After Taurus, which searches for peace and contentment in nature, comes the mutable air sign of Gemini, always looking for greener pastures. The motto "I think" conveys this sign's positive, highly intellectual side which is able to handle many ideas and activities at once. This is an active, restless, curious sign always involved in verbal communication and searching for variety and novelty.

Cancer: June 22–July 22
The Pieces: Water element, cardinal quality, feminine polarity.

The Picture: Cancer's motto "I feel" reveals its active quality and emotional element. Cancer must actively do something about its feelings: either turn them outward to nurture and protect others or turn inward to protect itself. The reflective feminine polarity tends to avoid confrontations; however, clever self-protective Cancer often uses powerful *in*sight into the emotional needs of others to make a profit.

Leo: July 23–August 22
The Pieces: Fire element, fixed quality, masculine polarity.

The Picture: This is the true "star" of the zodiac, burning with steady fixed fire, and commanding the attention of others. Leo is a "big" thinker, a confident and courageous doer whose motto is "I will." This generous sign loves to spread its warmth to others. It can be charismatic and dramatic; yet Leo also understands how to please its audience.

Virgo: August 23–September 22
The Pieces: Earth element, mutable quality, feminine polarity.

The Picture: Virgo is a reactor, whose earth element demands usefulness, while its mutable quality requires constant activity. It's no wonder that Virgo is known as the sign of work and service and finds fulfillment in this area. Virgo is the constant critic who picks things apart to make them work better. It is an organizer par excellence, who gets things done, though it is never quite satisfied. It's motto is "I analyze."

Libra: September 23–October 23
The Pieces: Air element, cardinal quality, masculine polarity.

The Picture: The mental character of this active positive air sign is expressed by the motto "I balance." Libra is a critical sign, but unlike Virgo, it is interested in an ideal perfection rather than usefulness; form precedes function. This sign is constantly weighing standards against an ideal of beauty, of justice, of peace and harmony. And though it remains unbiased and impartial, Libra often remains uncommitted.

Scorpio: October 24–November 21
The Pieces: Water element, fixed quality, feminine polarity.

The Picture: After the mental indecisive Libra, comes all-or-nothing Scorpio. This is the "still water" sign of the zodiac, deeply and fixedly emotional. Scorpio never wavers once it feels strongly about something or someone. Its motto is "I desire." Therefore anything under the sign of Scorpio is done passionately, with commitment. Unlike Libra, there are extreme highs and lows under this sign, since its intensity invariably throws things off balance. However there is great power of perception and a fascination for mysteries. This is a sign

21

meant to probe the depths and underlying secrets of human experience.

Sagittarius: November 22–December 21
The Pieces: Fire element, mutable quality, masculine polarity.

The Picture: Another restless mutable sign, fiery Sagittarius desires to ignite or inspire others. Its positive, masculine polarity gives it an outgoing gadabout nature. In this sign, fire spreads rapidly; so Sagittarius concerns itself with philosophy, religion, sales—spreading the "word." High aims for reaching universal truths are expressed in the motto "I aspire." Mutable Sagittarius needs to move physically to function well and often travels to far-distant places.

Capricorn: December 22–January 19
The Pieces: Earth element, cardinal quality, feminine polarity.

The Picture: Earth combined with the active cardinal quality makes Capricorn concerned with building, organizing, making material things happen. Capricorns are producers who work hard to achieve their high goals. The negative feminine polarity gives this sign the inner strength and discipline to attain power. Hardworking and conservative, Capricorn creates order by following rules and regulations, qualities expressed by the key words: "I utilize."

Aquarius: January 20–February 19
The Pieces: Air element, fixed quality, masculine polarity

The Picture: This fixed air combination clues us that Aquarius is a sign of principles, whose motto is "I know." It believes in absolutes that apply to all mankind, it relates to those in all walks of life and of all races. Aquarius is also interested in community goals and moving the masses toward a better way of life. Thus Aquarius is the most political sign. However, it acts on its ideas unswayed by other opinions. Therefore Aquarius may often espouse unorthodox or radical causes. And because it follows its own drummer, it is often far ahead of the pack.

Pisces: February 20–March 20
The Pieces: Water element, mutable quality, feminine polarity.

The Picture: The sensitive mutable antennae of Pisces operates in the emotional element of water. It is a restless, spiritual sign whose motto is "I believe" and whose frequent disregard of material reality often gives the sign a dreamy, otherworldly aura. Pisces finds fulfillment by expressing emotions artistically or by helping others, alleviating human suffering. This sign's negative polarity absorbs the feelings of those around it, requiring periods of solitude to replenish and center itself again. Since it is the most intuitive and compassionate sign, Pisceans can be of great service to humanity when they find a creative outlet.

3

The Sun:
Summing Up the *Outer* You

When most people speak of their astrological sign, they refer to their sun sign. "I'm a Taurus" means that the sun was passing through the part of the sky ruled by Taurus at the time you were born. So Taurus will play the leading role in your astrological drama, even though many other actors are involved in your horoscope, including nine other planets.

The placement of the sun is the first thing an astrologer wants to determine because it symbolizes your life force, ego, will, creativity, identity, spirit and consciousness. It is your *outgoing* energy, your basic astrological personality. The general horoscopes in magazines and newspapers are all based on the sun sign.

The sun colors the horoscope so strongly that, in most cases, you can make an amazingly accurate description of someone when you know nothing more than that person's sun sign. It's an easy way to analyze many people quickly and get important clues about human nature. Later, the other planets will enable you to delve more deeply adding individual details and shades of meaning to the "sun" picture.

In the absence of complete astrological data, you can

profit from knowing the general sun sign traits when your December-born boss frankly points out your shortcomings, when your Libran husband can't make a decision, or your Gemini wife flirts with every man at the party. You'll know that the tendency to bluntness, or to ponder every angle of a problem, or to exercise one's charm on everyone present are particular sun sign traits, and you'll handle them with ease.

When the sun is in harmony with other planets, its positive qualities are reinforced. Here are some of the gifts and talents at your disposal:

Sun in Aries
Pioneering spirit, courage, physical strength, aggressiveness, competitiveness, enthusiasm, fearlessness.

Watch out for: impatience, a tendency to leap before you look, disregard for the consequences of your actions.

Sun in Taurus
Patience, loyalty, stamina, sensuality, conservatism, good money sense, perseverance, artistic talent, green thumb.

Watch out for: stubbornness, a stick-in-the-mud attitude, reluctance to accept change or take chances, lack of spontaneity.

Sun in Gemini
Communications skill, versatility, writing ability, manual and mental dexterity, intelligence, adaptability, gift of gab, salesmanship.

Watch out for: too much talk and little action, rampant flirtatiousness, promiscuity, insensitivity to others' feelings, superficiality.

Sun in Cancer
Sensitivity, maternal instinct, good business sense, psychic ability, home-related skills, tenacity, empathy.

Watch out for: self-pity, using emotional manipulation, whining, a negative attitude, over-possessiveness, inability to take criticism, taking matters too personally.

Sun in Leo
A great sense of drama, theatrical talents, generosity, dignity, romanticism, pride, leadership abilities, flair and style.

Watch out for: bragging, believing flattery, indolence, choosing sycophantic companions, overspending, flashiness, monopolizing center stage, jealousy.

Sun in Virgo
Health-related talents, eye for design and detail, organizational ability, fastidiousness, criticism, good work habits, punctuality.

Watch out for: nagging, over-criticism, over-perfectionism, demanding others conform to your standards, intolerance, isolation.

Sun in Libra
Fairness, unselfishness, aesthic judgment, diplomacy, legal talents, good teamwork, creativity, matchmaking, sociability.

Watch out for: indecisiveness, vanity, going for beauty rather than substance, argumentativeness, avoiding emotional situations.

Sun in Scorpio
Insight, resourcefulness, regenerative ability, medical-related skills, detective ability, scientific talent, ability to cope in a crisis, stamina, persistence.

Watch out for: extremism, possessiveness, negativity, domineering tendencies, selfish sexual attitudes, attraction to the dark side of life, jealousy, inability to compromise.

Sun in Sagittarius
Optimism, independence, sales ability, theoretical mind, social skills, adaptability, love of travel, love of animals and the outdoors, a truth seeker.

Watch out for: tactlessness, rudeness, overspending, lack of refinement, recklessness, impatience, superficiality, overselling, gambling.

Sun in Capricorn
Discipline, organizational skills, executive ability, dedication, stamina, ambition, caution, seriousness of purpose, ability to use talents well.

Watch out for: opportunism, coldness, social climbing, snobbism, ruthlessness, workaholism.

Sun in Aquarius
Inventiveness, originality, group consciousness, idealism, understanding of mass power, detachment, inquisitive innovative mind.

Watch out for: fear of closeness, insensitivity, fame-worshipping, over-eccentricity, impersonality, hiding behind a cause.

Sun in Pisces
Compassion, artistic talent, psychic abilities, sensitivity, spirituality, imagination.

Watch out for: escapism, unwillingness to face reality, gullibility, depression, attraction to sob stories, self-pity, tendency to drown your sorrows.

The sun's position in the sky at the time you were born also affects how it works in your horoscope. In general, those born when the sun was above the horizon (in the daytime) tend to be more outgoing and lead a more public life than those born in the evening hours.

If you were born when the sun was rising, say 4–6 a.m., you have the full impact of your sun sign's outer expression. You sunrisers have a vivid personality and a powerful sense of your own identity—a double dose of magnetism. That's why you're often called a "double Taurus" or a "double Virgo."

Those born in the calm, late-night hours, approximately 2–4 a.m., are security and material-minded. Financial gain and possessions may come more easily to you. At any rate, you are a good manager of funds and will often have a position of importance dealing with or handling money.

If you took your first breath sometime between midnight and 2 a.m., you will express the communicative talents of your sign. Your emphasis is on curiosity and flexibility; you're a good talker, listener and writer.

Being born between 10 p.m. and midnight gives you an emphasis on home and the family. You may like to work at home or in a homelike environment. You'll enjoy making a warm, comforting home for your loved ones. As the sun is farthest away from the center of sky, you are a very private person; you may prefer to avoid the limelight, work behind the scenes. And success may come to you later in life.

If you were born between 8 and 10 p.m. you'll live out the creative aspect of your sun sign. Pleasure, play and affairs of the heart will keep your life dramatic and eventful. With your optimistic outlook, you'll make the best of this placement.

Those born between 6 and 8 p.m. have the craftsman-like aspect of your sun. Your instincts may lead you to activities that give service to others. And your life may involve many caretaking details. However, you can accomplish much by using your sun's organizational talents.

The sunset time of 4–6 p.m. gives you a need to share with others. You'll be drawn to partnerships and marriage and be powerfully influenced by those close to you. Hopefully, your sun will be in a cooperative sign (such as Libra) rather than the more independent signs (such as Aries). In any case, close relationships give a great deal of meaning to your life.

Those born from 2–4 p.m. may find yourself attracted to the healing arts, to matters of life and death. You're a great investigator, a mystic fascinated by life's mysteries. You have a strong, sexy body with great endurance. This position adds depth to your sun sign.

The sun high in the sky gives those born noon and 2 p.m. great aspirations. Not the domestic type, you'll be attracted to travel, religion, philosophy and seeking new experiences. You'll have strong opinions and make them known to others. You'll be concerned about your education and may go on to higher studies. Noontime births often draw people to seek worldly recognition for their activities. You look for the biggest audience.

Those born before noon, from 10 to 12 o'clock, will project the public image of their sun sign. It's important for you to find positive ways to express yourself. The right career choice puts you on a sure road to success and possibly fame. Make the most of your out-going nature.

The morning people, born from 8 to 10 a.m., have high hopes. You are a "people" person, and those grouped around you will have special importance. You're a liberal thinker and a good team player who identifies strongly with groups, social sets, political parties or causes that help the less fortunate. You need to find the right "team" for your particular talents.

The early morning people, born from 6 to 8 a.m., are challenged to grow in a spiritual way. This position gives you power, but it can also give you frustration because practical considerations often put a snag in your plans. You may not get to use your power to its fullest. At some point, you may feel confined, or be attracted to work at a spiritual retreat, hospital or prison. You can cope most constructively by finding a way to serve humanity—perhaps with your special acting talent or by helping others with emotional problems.

4

The Moon: Unlocking
Your Inner Secrets

As the sun represents the outer you, the moon's position in the zodiac at the time you were born reveals the inner feeling side of you, including your ups and downs, what you need to be happy, what you respond to emotionally in all areas of life. It affects your surroundings, what kind of home makes you feel most comfortable, what colors you respond to, your favorite foods. Anything having to do with a *need* is influenced by your moon sign.

Because the moon shines by *reflected* light, it follows that the moon is the passive receptacle of our impressions and memories. And as such, it rules your past, particularly instincts connected with your earliest childhood and your mother. In a woman's horoscope it tells how she feels about being a mother and a nurturer. In a man's horoscope, the moon represents the important woman in his life, the one he needs for emotional nurturing.

Particularly fascinating is the moon's sway on the subconscious side of our personalities, the mysterious intuitive self that operates on instincts rather than reason.

The moon rules the experience of those "gut-level" feelings that you can never quite explain rationally.

Obviously, because it governs the emotions, the moon is very important in romantic relationships. Knowing your partner's moon placement gives you clues to what he or she really needs, to whether your lover is easily hurt or made jealous, and to what you can do to satisfy that person emotionally.

A harmonious relationship between one partner's moon and key planets in the other person's chart augurs well for future happiness. It's logical that, when your moon is in the same sign as your loved one's moon, you should have similar emotional natures. This is especially important if your sun signs do not relate easily. In that case, your emotional twinship would offer you an all-important channel of communication.

Moons in different signs of the same element—two different earth signs, Capricorn and Taurus, for instance—will support each other and not have to work at emotional understanding. Moons in complementary elements—fire with air or earth with water—will also communicate emotionally. But if your moon is in a fire or air sign and your partner's is in earth or water, you'll have to make considerable effort to understand each other's feelings. You may often inadvertently ruffle each other's feathers. "How could he get upset over that silly little thing!" is a common refrain.

Moon compatibility is a key factor in the success of any relationship where emotions are involved. It can help offset many other difficulties because, regardless of the circumstances, you are able to sense and touch a responsive inner chord in each other—you'll find a way to communicate.

How do you find your moon placement? You must know the exact time of your birth, as well as the date and place, because the moon changes signs about every two days. For instance, if you were born on December

6 in a year when the moon was in Aries in the morning and changed into Taurus in the early afternoon, you'd want to be very sure of your birth time. A moon in Aries has different needs and feelings than a Taurus moon, even though your sun sign nature would remain Sagittarian. The fiery Aries moon would give extra emotional drive to the outgoing Sagittarian sun, but the Taurus moon would put emotional brakes on the risk-taking Sagittarius nature, bringing it down to earth.

The best way to find your moon placement is to consult a book of tables called an "ephemeris," which you can find at any astrological bookstore. This book charts the position of the moon and all the other planets for every day starting in 1900. Unfortunately moon tables are too long to print in this book.

Another alternative is to get a computer horoscope of your birth day or to have a professional astrologer do your horoscope. A third way to read the following moon sign descriptions and see which ones most resemble your inner feelings. If you feel you are not a true representative of your sun sign ("I somehow don't feel like a true Leo"), your moon sign may be affecting you strongly.

The moon is more forceful in some astrological signs than in others. It is the strongest in Cancer, which it rules. People with this placement will be super-sensitive to the moon's phases and really get emotional on the full moon.

Read through these descriptions to see which one most applies to you.

Moon in Aries
This is an active, hotheaded moon, a real dynamo. You're quick to be up and going and impatient with those who take their time. You're a risk taker who knows no fear. You're constantly after new experiences;

it's the chase, the quest that excites you. In love, you fall in and out quickly. You love the challenge of the unattainable. You may often get into battles of the sexes, particularly if your loved one tries to boss you around. Try to find a real partner you can respect who won't try to run your life.

You can't live without: action, a challenge.

Moon in Taurus

You're not after the pie in the sky; you need your goodies here and now. Things that are secure and lasting have solid appeal. Once you have whatever, or whomever, you need, that thing or person becomes your property, and no trespassing! This is a passionate, sensual moon. Fickle or flirtatious lovers are not for you. You're a slow starter, not easily upset; for this reason, others may lean on you for solid advice and comfort. Your surroundings should be soothing, close to nature, with lots of green growing things.

You can't live without: tangible pleasures.

Moon in Gemini

This is a restless moon that feels and loves with its mind. You need constant mental stimulation. You're more likely to cause jealousy than to be jealous. Not one for profound passion, you keep life interesting—and lovers on their toes—by doing many things at once, with many people. A constant change of scenery and cast of characters keeps you interested. The worst thing for you: any kind of solitary confinement.

You can't live without: variety, mental stimulation.

Moon in Cancer

The strongest moon of all needs to nurture others, to "mother the world." Your home is so important that you may never leave, always working from home base. This is a close, personal moon, that is very sensitive to criticism. You need someone who makes you feel secure and loved. That person should also be able to cope with your frequent changes of mood, especially at the full moon. No flirts for you! You tend to be possessive and to mother your loved ones. Be careful not to smother them. It's a good idea to cultivate positive-thinking friends.

You can't live without: a secure home base, someone to take care of.

Moon in Leo
The moon in this sun-ruled sign takes the lead in emotional situations. You are very proud and need the respect of others and will pay for deference from them with kindness and generosity. You take everything to heart and often need to put your love on a romantic pedestal. You also demand total attention from your beloved and hopefully get the royal treatment. Infidelity and stinginess are not tolerated. You also tend to be stubborn, reluctant to compromise or change your ways—you feel you know what's best.

You can't live without: admiration, respect.

Moon in Virgo
This is a picky moon who often has a tough time finding others who live up to your standards. You don't fall in love easily. You need to be more tolerant and accepting of imperfections. You demand physical and emotional order in your environment. You may drive others crazy picking up after them. You prudently prepare for all eventualities and get irritated when the unpredictable happens.

You can't live without: a sense of order, cleanliness.

Moon in Libra
You are forever questioning and testing to bring things better into balance. You hate anything that is out of

sync. You are susceptible to physical beauty, elegance and style and seek out a peaceful atmosphere in which to live. You need to share your life with others, so an active social life is important. Emotionally, you like to keep it light, no sticky scenes, please! You'll avoid confrontations which can't be resolved diplomatically.

You can't live without: a harmonious atmosphere.

Moon in Scorpio
This is a moon that has to get to the bottom of things. You'll probe the depths of emotion, unafraid of what you'll find there. Single-minded, you're not one to shun dramatic confrontations or scenes. Your feelings can easily go to extremes. You generally know exactly what you want and don't like to compromise. It's all or nothing. You need to be totally involved, so stay away from lighthearted lovers. It's also a good idea to channel some of that emotional drive into your work.

You can't live without: controlling the situation.

Moon in Sagittarius
Love them and leave them could be the motto of this restless fiery moon sign. All's well if you can find an equally independent partner, a happy-go-lucky traveling companion through life. You need lots of movement, fun and games and a lighthearted attitude. And above all you should not be fenced in, mentally or physically. You need to be free to follow exotic, highminded goals religions or philosophies.

You can't live without: freedom.

Moon in Capricorn
This is a discriminating moon that takes feelings seriously and needs the support of traditional institutions and commitment. That may be because you work hard and haven't time for frivolity, at least in your early years. You're the essence of upward mobility and you

need a partner who'll help you up the ladder of success. You may kick up your heels as you get older, after you've gotten what and where you want. But you'll always exercise discipline and self-control in expressing your emotions.

You can't live without: organization and "class."

Moon in Aquarius

You're constantly reaching out to others, yet you let few get really close. You need the feeling of being in contact with people and you're sensitive to their need to improve their lot. You'll have some unusual, highly original ways to help them. You tend to have quantities of friends and need a relationship with the masses. One-on-one emotional contact may make you uncomfortable. You'd rather analyze others' feelings from a distance. Not the jealous type, you often form unorthodox couplings.

You can't live without: friends, social contact with many groups.

Moon in Pisces

This is a sensitive impressionable moon that's a sucker for a sob story. Yours could be the shoulder everyone cries on. This moon make you absorb all the emotional vibes around you so be sure to let some successful, positive people into your life. You need to give lots of love and affection. You may also feel drawn to suffering humanity to the extent that you sacrifice your own best interests. Careful! Another no-no tendency: to feel sorry for yourself. Express your emotions romantically and creatively and find someone who has *your* best interests at heart!

You can't live without: romance, dreams.

How the Moon's Phases Affect Your Moods

You've heard of "moon madness," the Blue Moon, Harvest Moon and Silver Moon, not to mention Moonlight in Vermont and Over Miami. It's safe to say that more love songs have been written about the moon than any other theme, certainly any other planet! The full moon's emotional power has made us wax eloquent on paper and burst into song. The new moon has its fair share of publicity and we've even pondered "No Moon At All" musically.

This fascinating and powerful nighttime phenomena is epecially potent when reflected by the ocean. There, we can also contemplate the moon's gravitational pull on the ebb and flow of the tides and relate this to the fact that our own body is 90 percent water.

The belief in the moon's power over human, animal and plant behavior is almost as old as man himself. For many centuries the phases of the moon served as a celestial calendar. A body of folklore then grew around the phases of the moon. You can plant a garden, cut your hair, have an operation, predict the weather, start a business and of course fall in love according to favorable phases. There are other times when, according to moon lore, you'd better rest on your laurels. No matter how hard you try, nothing will be accomplished.

There's an old English belief that if Christmas comes during a waxing moon, the year will go well. However, if it falls during a waning moon, better be prepared for a year of testing and hard times. Here are some other lunar beliefs:

New moon on Monday is a sign of good luck.
A halo on the moon means a change of weather.
A misty moon is misfortune.
A new moon on Saturday means a long, rainy spell.

The full moon brings on criminal activity.

Children born on a full moon are stronger and wiser.

If a child is born on the waxing moon, the next child will be the same sex. On a waning moon, the next child will be the opposite sex.

Two full moons in a single calendar month bring floods and other calamities.

One thing we do know for sure, the moon was probably the first heavenly body to be related to human behavior, and to start the "love affair" with astrology that has continued through the ages.

When we contemplate the reasons for a full moon, some of the emotional connections begin to make sense. The full moon happens when the sun is directly opposite, creating a pull between these two bodies (with the earth in the middle). The moon now reflects the most light from the sun. So this is the time when matters come to a head, when emotional problems surface, when we feel "pulled apart." How many lovers have finally confessed their feelings under the full moon! How many acts of violence from repressed rage burst forth! Even oysters open widest when the full moon is directly overhead.

The new moon occurs when the sun and the moon are in the same part of the sky, viewed from our vantage point on earth. The moon comes between the earth and the sun, with both powerful bodies pulling in the same direction. So it follows that this augurs well for starting things, for making plans for the future. With everything "pulling" for you now, you will have a clear sense of purpose.

The full moon will also affect you according to the astrological sign it is in. Bear in mind that, since the moon is now opposite the sun, it will fall in the sign that is farthest away from the sun in the zodiac. So, when the sun is in Aries, the full moon will be in Libra, its astrological opposite. A full moon will be especially potent for you if it affects your sun sign, in the above case, if you are an Aries or a Libra. You'll also feel some tension if your sign is midway between Aries and Libra—if you are a Capricorn or a Cancer.

Each full moon takes on the special characteristics of its sign. Here's what to expect from the full moons of 1988.

Full Moon in Aries (September 25):
This is an explosive full moon where impatience runs high. People are out to get their own way. They may jump into things without looking at the consequences. This is especially true of romance. Don't believe everything you hear—wait a while. Also watch accidents and fires. Those in the combat zone will be Aries, Libra, Capricorn and Cancer.

Full Moon in Taurus (October 24)
This is a sexy sensual full moon. You'll really feel the magnetism of the opposite sex. You'll have strong appetites and be tempted to overindulge. It will be difficult to stay on a diet. On the negative side, watch your possessions. Keep your wallet well-hidden. Those affected most will be Scorpio, Taurus, Leo and Aquarius.

Full Moon in Gemini (November 23)
This full moon makes everyone agitated and extra-talkative. It's a great time for a party, for making telephone calls, dashing off letters. There could be a bit too much going on; you may feel pulled in many different directions. Stop to think before you make a committment now. Better wait a few days. Romantically, you may find yourself attracted to two people, or tempted to stray from a steady love. Especially agitated will be Geminis, Pisces, Sagittarius and Virgo.

Full Moon in Cancer (January 3 and December 23)
This is the soggiest, most emotional full moon. You may feel very sorry for yourself, like staying safe at home. Your best bet is to cook a terrific meal for those you love, spend some time with children or go for a boat trip. This goes particularly for Cancer, Capricorn, Aries and Libra.

Full Moon in Leo (February 2)
This is a jolly full moon that's great for a romantic summer party. Treat your lover like a king or queen, but watch a tendency to overspend. And be careful of tender egos. They may need extra shoring up now. Attention: Leo, Aquarius, Taurus and Scorpio.

Full Moon in Virgo (March 3—Eclipse)
If you've been postponing those little details of life or housecleaning activities, now's the time to put your life in order. Disorganization will provoke arguments today, especially for Pisces, Virgo, Sagittarius and Gemini. Time to shape up health-wise too. Don't postpone checkups; join a gym.

Full Moon in Libra (April 2)
The challenge today is to stay in balance. Watch out for legal tangles. It may be difficult to make decisions today—one part of you wants to race ahead, the other part of you puts on the brakes. Better to socialize with friends you enjoy in lovely surroundings. This goes for Libra, Aries, Capricorn and Cancer.

Full Moon in Scorpio (May 1)
Watch those crimes of passion, jealousy and revenge come to light! If life is a bit rocky, better sit this full moon out. Plan some sexy happenings at home. Try to

keep calm and cool in other situations. Take note Scorpio, Taurus, Leo and Aquarius.

Full Moon in Sagittarius (May 31)
You may be tempted to take a gamble. Be sure the odds are in your favor. Others may not be acting responsibly today. You may find lots more talk than action. It's better to spend time outdoors, at your favorite sporting event or just walking the dog. It's also a good time for a party, Gemini, Sagittarius, Pisces or Virgo.

Full Moon in Capricorn (June 29)
Your relationship may need work today. People are taking life very seriously, especially financial matters. It's a good time to pay attention to older folks and to traditional duties. Take note Capricorn, Cancer, Aries and Libra.

Full Moon in Aquarius (July 29)
This is a friendly full moon when you'll feel a special need to reach out. This is a good time for socializing, for doing things in large groups. Intimate relationships may cool off temporarily, while you concentrate on the big picture. Be sure that you don't step on someone's toes with a shocking remark. And watch your electrical gadgets. Those affected most will be Scorpio, Aquarius, Leo and Taurus.

Full Moon in Pisces (August 27—Eclipse)
You are highly sensitive today—you may feel like drowning your sorrows, so watch your alcoholic intake. Better to escape via an artistic route. Lift your mood with music and dancing. Or commiserate in good company. There will be lots of sob stories afloat. Pisces, Virgo, Sagittarius and Gemini will be extra touchy.

Moon Positions—1988

These placements were calculated from *American Ephemeris for the Twentieth Century* (Neil F. Michelson-ACS Publications) The times were adjusted for Eastern Standard Time.

Friday, January 1 — Moon in Gemini

Saturday, January 2 — Moon in Gemini to Cancer 7:15 p.m.

Sunday, January 3 — Moon in Cancer

Monday, January 4 — Moon in Cancer

Tuesday, January 5 — Moon in Cancer to Leo 6:47 a.m.

Wednesday, January 6 — Moon in Leo

Thursday, January 7 — Moon in Leo to Virgo 7:35 p.m.

Friday, January 8 — Moon in Virgo

Saturday, January 9 — Moon in Virgo

Sunday, January 10 — Moon in Virgo to Libra 8:17 a.m.

Monday, January 11 — Moon in Libra

Tuesday, January 12 — Moon in Libra to Scorpio 6:39 p.m.

Wednesday, January 13 — Moon in Scorpio

Thursday, January 14 — Moon in Scorpio to Sagittarius 12:58 a.m.

Friday, January 15 — Moon in Sagittarius

Saturday, January 16 — Moon in Sagittarius

Sunday, January 17 — Moon in Sagittarius to Capricorn 3:15 a.m.

Monday, January 18 — Moon in Capricorn

Tuesday, January 19 — Moon in Capricorn to Aquarius 3:02 a.m.

Wednesday, January 20 — Moon in Aquarius

Thursday, January 21 — Moon in Aquarius to Pisces 2:27 a.m.

Friday, January 22 — Moon in Pisces

Saturday, January 23 — Moon in Pisces to Aries 3:31 a.m.

Sunday, January 24	Moon in Aries
Monday, January 25	Moon in Aries to Taurus 7:36 a.m.
Tuesday, January 26	Moon in Taurus
Wednesday, January 27	Moon in Taurus to Gemini 3:02 p.m.
Thursday, January 28	Moon in Gemini
Friday, January 29	Moon in Gemini
Saturday, January 30	Moon in Gemini to Cancer 1:11 a.m.
Sunday, January 31	Moon in Cancer
Monday, February 1	Moon in Cancer to Leo 1:06 p.m.
Tuesday, February 2	Moon in Leo
Wednesday, February 3	Moon in Leo
Thursday, February 4	Moon in Leo to Virgo 1:54 a.m.
Friday, February 5	Moon in Virgo
Saturday, February 6	Moon in Virgo to Libra 2:36 p.m.
Sunday, February 7	Moon in Libra
Monday, February 8	Moon in Libra
Tuesday, February 9	Moon in Libra to Scorpio 1:42 a.m.
Wednesday, February 10	Moon in Scorpio
Thursday, February 11	Moon in Scorpio to Sagittarius 9:36 a.m.
Friday, February 12	Moon in Sagittarius
Saturday, February 13	Moon in Sagittarius to Capricorn 1:36 p.m.
Sunday, February 14	Moon in Capricorn
Monday, February 15	Moon in Capricorn to Aquarius 2:25 p.m.
Tuesday, February 16	Moon in Aquarius
Wednesday, February 17	Moon in Aquarius to Pisces 1:44 p.m.
Thursday, February 18	Moon in Pisces
Friday, February 19	Moon in Pisces to Aries 1:35 p.m.
Saturday, February 20	Moon in Aries
Sunday, February 21	Moon in Aries to Taurus 3:50 p.m.

Monday, February 22	Moon in Taurus
Tuesday, February 23	Moon in Taurus to Gemini 9:42 p.m.
Wednesday, February 24	Moon in Gemini
Thursday, February 25	Moon in Gemini
Friday, February 26	Moon in Cancer 7:12 a.m.
Saturday, February 27	Moon in Cancer
Sunday, February 28	Moon in Cancer to Leo 7:12 p.m.
Monday, February 29	Moon in Leo
Tuesday, March 1	Moon in Leo
Wednesday, March 2	Moon in Leo to Virgo 8:06 a.m.
Thursday, March 3	Moon in Virgo
Friday, March 4	Moon in Virgo to Libra 8:32 p.m.
Saturday, March 5	Moon in Libra
Sunday, March 6	Moon in Libra
Monday, March 7	Moon in Libra to Scorpio 7:27 a.m.
Tuesday, March 8	Moon in Scorpio
Wednesday, March 9	Moon in Scorpio to Sagittarius 3:59 p.m.
Thursday, March 10	Moon in Sagittarius
Friday, March 11	Moon in Sagittarius to Capricorn 9:31 p.m.
Saturday, March 12	Moon in Capricorn
Sunday, March 13	Moon in Capricorn
Monday, March 14	Moon in Capricorn to Aquarius 12:08 a.m.
Tuesday, March 15	Moon in Aquarius
Wednesday, March 16	Moon in Aquarius to Pisces 12:42 a.m.
Thursday, March 17	Moon in Pisces
Friday, March 18	Moon in Pisces to Aries 12:45 a.m.
Saturday, March 19	Moon in Aries
Sunday, March 20	Moon in Aries to Taurus 2:05 a.m.

Monday, March 21	Moon in Taurus
Tuesday, March 22	Moon in Taurus to Gemini 6:21 a.m.
Wednesday, March 23	Moon in Gemini
Thursday, March 24	Moon in Gemini to Cancer 2:27 p.m.
Friday, March 25	Moon in Cancer
Saturday, March 26	Moon in Cancer
Sunday, March 27	Moon in Cancer to Leo 1:54 a.m.
Monday, March 28	Moon in Leo
Tuesday, March 29	Moon in Leo to Virgo 2:49 p.m.
Wednesday, March 30	Moon in Virgo
Thursday, March 31	Moon in Virgo
Friday, April 1	Moon in Virgo to Libra 3:05 a.m.
Saturday, April 2	Moon in Libra
Sunday, April 3	Moon in Libra to Scorpio 1:26 p.m.
Monday, April 4	Moon in Scorpio
Tuesday, April 5	Moon in Scorpio to Sagittarius 9:29 p.m.
Wednesday, April 6	Moon in Sagittarius
Thursday, April 7	Moon in Sagittarius
Friday, April 8	Moon in Sagittarius to Capricorn 3:19 a.m.
Saturday, April 9	Moon in Capricorn
Sunday, April 10	Moon in Capricorn to Aquarius 7:10 a.m.
Monday, April 11	Moon in Aquarius
Tuesday, April 12	Moon in Aquarius to Pisces 9:24 a.m.
Wednesday, April 13	Moon in Pisces
Thursday, April 14	Moon in Pisces to Aries 10:47 a.m.
Friday, April 15	Moon in Aries
Saturday, April 16	Moon in Aries to Taurus 12:31 p.m.

Sunday, April 17	Moon in Taurus
Monday, April 18	Moon in Taurus to Gemini 4:10 p.m.
Tuesday, April 19	Moon in Gemini
Wednesday, April 20	Moon in Gemini to Cancer 11:04 p.m.
Thursday, April 21	Moon in Cancer
Friday, April 22	Moon in Cancer
Saturday, April 23	Moon in Cancer to Leo 9:34 a.m.
Sunday, April 24	Moon in Leo
Monday, April 25	Moon in Leo to Virgo 10:16 p.m.
Tuesday, April 26	Moon in Virgo
Wednesday, April 27	Moon in Virgo
Thursday, April 28	Moon in Virgo to Libra 10:37 a.m.
Friday, April 29	Moon in Libra
Saturday, April 30	Moon in Libra to Scorpio 8:39 a.m.
Sunday, May 1	Moon in Scorpio
Monday, May 2	Moon in Scorpio
Tuesday, May 3	Moon in Scorpio to Sagittarius 3:52 a.m.
Wednesday, May 4	Moon in Sagittarius
Thursday, May 5	Moon in Sagittarius to Capricorn 8:54 a.m.
Friday, May 6	Moon in Capricorn
Saturday, May 7	Moon in Capricorn to Aquarius 12:37 p.m.
Sunday, May 8	Moon in Aquarius
Monday, May 9	Moon in Aquarius to Pisces 3:39 p.m.
Tuesday, May 10	Moon in Pisces
Wednesday, May 11	Moon in Pisces to Aries 6:23 p.m.
Thursday, May 12	Moon in Aries
Friday, May 13	Moon in Aries to Taurus 9:22 p.m.
Saturday, May 14	Moon in Taurus
Sunday, May 15	Moon in Taurus

Monday, May 16	Moon in Taurus to Gemini 1:31 a.m.
Tuesday, May 17	Moon in Gemini
Wednesday, May 18	Moon in Gemini to Cancer 8:05 a.m.
Thursday, May 19	Moon in Cancer
Friday, May 20	Moon in Cancer to Leo 5:51 p.m.
Saturday, May 21	Moon in Leo
Sunday, May 22	Moon in Leo
Monday, May 23	Moon in Leo to Virgo 6:12 a.m.
Tuesday, May 24	Moon in Virgo
Wednesday, May 25	Moon in Virgo to Libra 6:49 p.m.
Thursday, May 26	Moon in Libra
Friday, May 27	Moon in Libra
Saturday, May 28	Moon in Libra to Scorpio 5:06 a.m.
Sunday, May 29	Moon in Scorpio
Monday May 30	Moon in Scorpio to Sagittarius 11:57 a.m.
Tuesday, May 31	Moon in Sagittarius
Wednesday, June 1	Moon in Sagittarius to Capricorn 3:59 p.m.
Thursday, June 2	Moon in Capricorn
Friday, June 3	Moon in Capricorn to Aquarius 6:34 p.m.
Saturday, June 4	Moon in Aquarius
Sunday, June 5	Moon in Aquarius to Pisces 9 p.m.
Monday, June 6	Moon in Pisces
Tuesday, June 7	Moon in Pisces
Wednesday, June 8	Moon in Pisces to Aries 12:04 a.m.
Thursday, June 9	Moon in Aries
Friday, June 10	Moon in Aries to Taurus 4:02 a.m.
Saturday, June 11	Moon in Taurus
Sunday, June 12	Moon in Taurus to Gemini 9:14 a.m.
Monday, June 13	Moon in Gemini

Tuesday, June 14	Moon in Gemini to Cancer 4:19 p.m.
Wednesday, June 15	Moon in Cancer
Thursday, June 16	Moon in Cancer
Friday, June 17	Moon in Cancer to Leo 1:57 a.m.
Saturday, June 18	Moon in Leo
Sunday, June 19	Moon in Leo to Virgo 2:03 p.m.
Monday, June 20	Moon in Virgo
Tuesday, June 21	Moon in Virgo
Wednesday, June 22	Moon in Virgo to Libra 2:57 a.m.
Thursday, June 23	Moon in Libra
Friday, June 24	Moon in Libra to Scorpio 1:58 p.m.
Saturday, June 25	Moon in Scorpio
Sunday, June 26	Moon in Scorpio to Sagittarius 9:18 p.m.
Monday, June 27	Moon in Sagittarius
Tuesday, June 28	Moon in Sagittarius
Wednesday, June 29	Moon in Sagittarius to Capricorn 1 a.m.
Thursday, June 30	Moon in Capricorn
Friday, July 1	Moon in Capricorn to Aquarius 2:30 a.m.
Saturday, July 2	Moon in Aquarius
Sunday, July 3	Moon in Aquarius to Pisces 3:33 a.m.
Monday, July 4	Moon in Pisces
Tuesday, July 5	Moon in Pisces to Aries 5:37 a.m.
Wednesday, July 6	Moon in Aries
Thursday, July 7	Moon in Aries to Taurus 9:27 a.m.
Friday, July 8	Moon in Taurus
Saturday, July 9	Moon in Taurus to Gemini 3:16 p.m.
Sunday, July 10	Moon in Gemini
Monday, July 11	Moon in Gemini to Cancer 11:08 p.m.

Tuesday, July 12	Moon in Cancer
Wednesday, July 13	Moon in Cancer
Thursday, July 14	Moon in Cancer to Leo 9:11 a.m.
Friday, July 15	Moon in Leo
Saturday, July 16	Moon in Leo to Virgo 9:17 p.m.
Sunday, July 17	Moon in Virgo
Monday, July 18	Moon in Virgo
Tuesday, July 19	Moon in Virgo to Libra 10:22 a.m.
Wednesday, July 20	Moon in Libra
Thursday, July 21	Moon in Libra to Scorpio 10:13 p.m.
Friday, July 22	Moon in Scorpio
Saturday, July 23	Moon in Scorpio
Sunday, July 24	Moon in Scorpio to Sagittarius 6:42 a.m.
Monday, July 25	Moon in Sagittarius
Tuesday, July 26	Moon in Sagittarius to Capricorn 11:07 a.m.
Wednesday, July 27	Moon in Capricorn
Thursday, July 28	Moon in Capricorn to Aquarius 12:25 p.m.
Friday, July 29	Moon in Aquarius
Saturday, July 30	Moon in Aquarius to Pisces 12:23 p.m.
Sunday, July 31	Moon in Pisces
Monday, August 1	Moon in Pisces to Aries 12:53 p.m.
Tuesday, August 2	Moon in Aries
Wednesday, August 3	Moon in Aries to Taurus 3:24 p.m.
Thursday, August 4	Moon in Taurus
Friday, August 5	Moon in Taurus to Gemini 8:43 p.m.
Saturday, August 6	Moon in Gemini
Sunday, August 7	Moon in Gemini
Monday, August 8	Moon in Gemini to Cancer 4:52 a.m.

Tuesday, August 9	Moon in Cancer
Wednesday, August 10	Moon in Cancer to Leo 3:26 p.m.
Thursday, August 11	Moon in Leo
Friday, August 12	Moon in Leo
Saturday, August 13	Moon in Leo to Virgo 3:46 a.m.
Sunday, August 14	Moon in Virgo
Monday, August 15	Moon in Virgo to Libra 4:52 p.m.
Tuesday, August 16	Moon in Libra
Wednesday, August 17	Moon in Libra
Thursday, August 18	Moon in Libra to Scorpio 5:12 a.m.
Friday, August 19	Moon in Scorpio
Saturday, August 20	Moon in Scorpio to Sagittarius 2:55 p.m.
Sunday, August 21	Moon in Sagittarius
Monday, August 22	Moon in Sagittarius to Capricorn 8:49 p.m.
Tuesday, August 23	Moon in Capricorn
Wednesday, August 24	Moon in Capricorn to Aquarius 11:05 p.m.
Thursday, August 25	Moon in Aquarius
Friday, August 26	Moon in Aquarius to Pisces 11:01 p.m.
Saturday, August 27	Moon in Pisces
Sunday, August 28	Moon in Pisces to Aries 10:29 p.m.
Monday, August 29	Moon in Aries
Tuesday, August 30	Moon in Aries to Taurus 11:22 p.m.
Wednesday, August 31	Moon in Taurus
Thursday, September 1	Moon in Taurus
Friday, September 2	Moon in Taurus to Gemini 3:11 a.m.
Saturday, September 3	Moon in Gemini
Sunday, September 4	Moon in Gemini to Cancer 10:37 a.m.
Monday, September 5	Moon in Cancer
Tuesday, September 6	Moon in Cancer to Leo 9:14 p.m.

Wednesday, September 7	Moon in Leo
Thursday, September 8	Moon in Leo
Friday, September 9	Moon in Leo to Virgo 9:48 a.m.
Saturday, September 10	Moon in Virgo
Sunday, September 11	Moon in Virgo to Libra 10:51 p.m.
Monday, September 12	Moon in Libra
Tuesday, September 13	Moon in Libra
Wednesday, September 14	Moon in Libra to Scorpio 11:07 a.m.
Thursday, September 15	Moon in Scorpio
Friday, September 16	Moon in Scorpio to Sagittarius 9:25 p.m.
Saturday, September 17	Moon in Sagittarius
Sunday, September 18	Moon in Sagittarius
Monday, September 19	Moon in Sagittarius to Capricorn 4:45 a.m.
Tuesday, September 20	Moon in Capricorn
Wednesday, September 21	Moon in Capricorn to Aquarius 8:43 a.m.
Thursday, September 22	Moon in Aquarius
Friday, September 23	Moon in Aquarius to Pisces 9:51 a.m.
Saturday, September 24	Moon in Pisces
Sunday, September 25	Moon in Pisces to Aries 9:29 a.m.
Monday, September 26	Moon in Aries
Tuesday, September 27	Moon in Aries to Taurus 9:29 a.m.
Wednesday, September 28	Moon in Taurus
Thursday, September 29	Moon in Taurus to Gemini 11:43 a.m.
Friday, September 30	Moon in Gemini
Saturday, October 1	Moon in Gemini to Cancer 5:39 p.m.
Sunday, October 2	Moon in Cancer
Monday, October 3	Moon in Cancer
Tuesday, October 4	Moon in Cancer to Leo 3:31 a.m.

Wednesday, October 5	Moon in Leo
Thursday, October 6	Moon in Leo to Virgo 4:01 p.m.
Friday, October 7	Moon in Virgo
Saturday, October 8	Moon in Virgo
Sunday, October 9	Moon in Virgo to Libra 5:03 a.m.
Monday, October 10	Moon in Libra
Tuesday, October 11	Moon in Libra to Scorpio 4:58 p.m.
Wednesday, October 12	Moon in Scorpio
Thursday, October 13	Moon in Scorpio
Friday, October 14	Moon in Scorpio to Sagittarius 2:58 a.m.
Saturday, October 15	Moon in Sagittarius
Sunday, October 16	Moon in Sagittarius to Capricorn 10:44 a.m.
Monday, October 17	Moon in Capricorn
Tuesday, October 18	Moon in Capricorn to Aquarius 4:05 p.m.
Wednesday, October 19	Moon in Aquarius
Thursday, October 20	Moon in Aquarius to Pisces 6:58 p.m.
Friday, October 21	Moon in Pisces
Saturday, October 22	Moon in Pisces to Aries 7:59 p.m.
Sunday, October 23	Moon in Aries
Monday, October 24	Moon in Aries to Taurus 8:22 p.m.
Tuesday, October 25	Moon in Taurus
Wednesday, October 26	Moon in Taurus to Gemini 9:55 p.m.
Thursday, October 27	Moon in Gemini
Friday, October 28	Moon in Gemini
Saturday, October 29	Moon in Gemini to Cancer 2:28 a.m.
Sunday, October 30	Moon in Cancer
Monday, October 31	Moon in Cancer to Leo 11:03 a.m.
Tuesday, November 1	Moon in Leo
Wednesday, November 2	Moon in Leo to Virgo 11:02 p.m.

Thursday, November 3	Moon in Virgo
Friday, November 4	Moon in Virgo
Saturday, November 5	Moon in Virgo to Libra 12:04 p.m.
Sunday, November 6	Moon in Libra
Monday, November 7	Moon in Libra to Scorpio 11:46 p.m.
Tuesday, November 8	Moon in Scorpio
Wednesday, November 9	Moon in Scorpio
Thursday, November 10	Moon in Scorpio to Sagittarius 9:06 a.m.
Friday, November 11	Moon in Sagittarius
Saturday, November 12	Moon in Sagittarius to Capricorn 4:12 p.m.
Sunday, November 13	Moon in Capricorn
Monday, November 14	Moon in Capricorn to Aquarius 9:36 p.m.
Tuesday, November 15	Moon in Aquarius
Wednesday, November 16	Moon in Aquarius
Thursday, November 17	Moon in Aquarius to Pisces 1:34 a.m.
Friday, November 18	Moon in Pisces
Saturday, November 19	Moon in Pisces to Aries 4:12 a.m.
Sunday, November 20	Moon in Aries
Monday, November 21	Moon in Aries to Taurus 6:02 a.m.
Tuesday, November 22	Moon in Taurus
Wednesday, November 23	Moon in Taurus to Gemini 8:12 a.m.
Thursday, November 24	Moon in Gemini
Friday, November 25	Moon in Gemini to Cancer 12:19 p.m.
Saturday, November 26	Moon in Cancer
Sunday, November 27	Moon in Cancer to Leo 7:52 p.m.
Monday, November 28	Moon in Leo
Tuesday, November 29	Moon in Leo
Wednesday, November 30	Moon in Leo to Virgo 7 a.m.

Thursday, December 1	Moon in Virgo
Friday, December 2	Moon in Virgo to Libra 7:56 p.m.
Saturday, December 3	Moon in Libra
Sunday, December 4	Moon in Libra
Monday, December 5	Moon in Libra to Scorpio 7:51 a.m.
Tuesday, December 6	Moon in Scorpio
Wednesday, December 7	Moon in Scorpio to Sagittarius 4:55 p.m.
Thursday, December 8	Moon in Sagittarius
Friday, December 9	Moon in Sagittarius to Capricorn 11:07 p.m.
Saturday, December 10	Moon in Capricorn
Sunday, December 11	Moon in Capricorn
Monday, December 12	Moon in Capricorn to Aquarius 3:25 a.m.
Tuesday, December 13	Moon in Aquarius
Wednesday, December 14	Moon in Aquarius to Pisces 6:53 a.m.
Thursday, December 15	Moon in Pisces
Friday, December 16	Moon in Pisces to Aries 10:03 a.m.
Saturday, December 17	Moon in Aries
Sunday, December 18	Moon in Aries to Taurus 1:11 p.m.
Monday, December 19	Moon in Taurus
Tuesday, December 20	Moon in Taurus to Gemini 4:43 p.m.
Wednesday, December 21	Moon in Gemini
Thursday, December 22	Moon in Gemini to Cancer 9:35 p.m.
Friday, December 23	Moon in Cancer
Saturday, December 24	Moon in Cancer
Sunday, December 25	Moon in Cancer to Leo 4:57 a.m.
Monday, December 26	Moon in Leo
Tuesday, December 27	Moon in Leo to Virgo 3:27 p.m.
Wednesday, December 28	Moon in Virgo
Thursday, December 29	Moon in Virgo
Friday, December 30	Moon in Virgo to Libra 4:09 a.m.
Saturday, December 31	Moon in Libra

5

Mercury, Venus and Mars: The Personal Planets

As we have seen, the sun and the moon in astrology represent the way you are, that is, your inner and outer energy. Now come the planets that deal with your relationships to others. Mercury governs how you communicate with others. Venus, the planet of love and beauty, shows what attracts you in other things and people, how you relate to others, what you *want* (rather than what you *need*, which is determined by the moon). Mars is your energy and drive, how you *do* things. It shows what motivates you, what will get you up and running and how you actively make love.

These planets affect your day-to-day dealings with others on every level. That includes how you go about contacting people, how well you express yourself, how you win them over and what appeals to you most— what turns you on.

In other words: Venus wants it (or her/him).

> Mars goes after it.
> Mercury talks about it.

Mercury—Your Gift of Gab

This speedy little planet was once thought to bring messages from the great sun down to earth. You might think of it as a buddy to the sun, or a handy errand boy who is always on call, never more than two signs away. This means you'll never find your Mercury in a sign opposite your sun sign, working against it.

Mercury is a mental planet that reflects your thinking, speaking and writing abilities. If it is in the same sign as your sun, it will reflect and reinforce your sun's mental attributes. If it is in a different sign, you will have the other sign's characteristics in your style of communicating. For instance, a Sagittarius with Mercury in Sagittarius might be blunt and direct to the point of rudeness. If that Sag's Mercury was in Scorpio, he or she would calculate the power of words and think before speaking. Placed two signs back in Libra, Mercury would give that Sag a far more diplomatic tongue, a super dose of charm.

Mercury rules and shines most brightly in the signs of Gemini and Virgo. Each expresses a different side of the planet's personality. Gemini is the social side, with great verbal skills, charm and a gift of gab that can literally talk itself into and out of any situation. It puts Mercury into the element of air and is known for communicating via the written word. In Gemini, Mercury spreads the word. Earth-sign Virgo brings out the practical side of the planet, concerned with analyzing and perfecting the way things work. It knows what is wrong and how to do things better. A Virgo with Mercury in Virgo is happiest when telling the world how to behave, what to do for its own good.

Like most hyperactive, high-strung people and things, Mercury has contrary irritable moods. It races around the sun in 88 days and, sometimes, when viewed from our slower pace on earth, it seems to move backward in the sky. When this happens, about three times a year, Mercury activities literally go haywire. Wires get crossed, telephones break down, messages are missed or misinterpreted. Commitments made at this time are particularly perilous. Contracts get broken, documents signed may be later regretted, lawsuits run into snags. This is the time to double-check everything, be sure to keep records and take clear messages. And try not to make commitments until Mercury grinds to a halt and pushes forward again, usually in about three weeks.

Your own Mercury tells you lots about how you communicate. Are you one for silent communication, sparkling repartee or deep philosophical discussions? Since the planet is either in your sun sign or two or three signs away (in either direction), you should be able to guess where your placement is by reading through the descriptions that follow. If you want the exact placement, you can look it up in a book of tables or have your horoscope computed.

Mercury in Aries

You come across as warm, friendly, energetic, interested in new ideas, a bit trendy. The flip side is that you may talk about yourself too much. You're a good debater, with a fast comeback, who loves a mental challenge. Arguments stimulate you. But you may tend to speak before you think, disregarding the listener's feelings. Sensitivity is not your strong point.

Mercury in Taurus

You may speak very slowly, with a rich, earthy quality to your voice. Chances are it is melodious. One is very conscious of its sound, in any case. You communicate best when you are negotiating, in the language of a trader. You're not one for cocktail party chitchat. You have good concentration and a thoroughness about all your mental activities.

Mercury in Gemini

You're one of the best talkers around. You can talk yourself into and out of anything. And you may never shut up. A desert island would be your worst vacation. You need a telephone with at least three lines. And you have them all working. The best thing: You're positive, unbiased and very good-humored. You may have a flair for foreign languages and dialects and be a great mimic.

Mercury in Cancer

This Mercury is more intuitive than mental. You know just how to get to people where they hurt or where they feel good. Using emotional language rather than logic, you can appeal to basic needs and sway many people this way. This placement gives a marvelous memory, perhaps a "photographic" one, with near total recall. You like deep discussions about feelings, emotional issues. Purely theoretical views rarely interest you. You can also use language to manipulate people emotionally— good for selling, acting and public speaking.

Mercury in Leo

You love to talk about yourself and brag about your accomplishments, but usually in a dignified way. This is a "me first" Mercury that can be a bit pompous. But you do know how to sell yourself and present yourself with confidence. You have good concentration and mental stamina. And your mind works well when directing others. You give orders easily with a natural authority. Watch a tendency to be too bossy and tread on others' tender feelings.

Mercury in Virgo

This is the most critical Mercury. You're a great student, teacher and writer, with a flair for details and an ability to put what you learn to practical use. You also may have a talent for medicine, or work in the health and diet fields. However, you are often the type who gets bogged down in details and can't see the forest for the trees. You can also be too skeptical and discriminating for your own good.

Mercury in Libra

You have great objectivity and reasoning capacity. You love to debate all sides of the question. You also have a great deal of charm and diplomacy, good social communications skills. You are not a loner. You function best in an association with others or in a partnership. The mental contact and stimulation of others inspire you.

Mercury in Scorpio

You have very strong, definite opinions and like to work by yourself, getting intensely involved in everything you do. Because you need total control of your projects, your mind functions best in solitary problem-solving work: science, psychology, design, detective work where you can delve beneath the surface of a situation. You have marvelous concentration and can be quite inventive. You are not a "group" person. One reason may be that you are quite secretive, though you do enjoy ferreting out the secrets of others. Superficial communication holds no appeal for you, and you are the master of the sarcastic, cutting comment that gets to the heart of the matter.

Mercury in Sagittarius

With this mentally active placement, you enjoy higher intellectual pursuits: philosophy, religion, science. You love to play with ideas, jumping from one subject to another. You may tend to change your mind and your job frequently, especially early in life. You are especially attracted to exotic ideas and concepts. You can't tolerate mental restrictions of any kind, which may make you rebellious. You are philosophical about everything, very generous and like to be in a position of authority, acting as advisor and mentor. Socially, you are outgoing and fun, with a great sense of humor and wonderful sales ability. You do insist on your right to speak the truth at all costs and your barbs often wound others' feelings.

Mercury in Capricorn
Rarely interested in study for its own sake, you look for ideas you can use, which will elevate your life-style and advance your career. You climb toward high goals and can see the overall picture in any situation. If it suits you, you can be extremely diplomatic and demonstrate a very classy way of presenting your ideas. This is the most organized mental placement, giving you great mental discipline and work habits. Socially, you can come across as a very serious, dignified type, perhaps a bit of a snob, yet you have a wonderful dry sense of humor.

Mercury in Aquarius
This is a high-tech placement, very interested in advanced ideas, finding new and original solutions to problems, using state-of-the-art equipment. You may be far ahead of your time, thus considered a bit of an oddball by others. Yet you have excellent concentration and reasoning powers, you enjoy the company of a wide range of people from all walks of life and social and economic levels. You probably have a diverse "collection" of friends, many of whom share your liberal humanitarian interests.

Mercury in Pisces
This is a deeply sympathetic Mercury that understands the needs of others. The knowledge you trust comes more from your intuitive impressions than from

books. You don't always know why you understand a situation. In a group, you can sense the thoughts of others. You have a great memory that absorbs facts quickly. You may be attracted to hospitals or other institutions where you can help others. Socially, you can be very witty, using words creatively; yet you are always tactful.

Venus—What Turns You On

Want to find out how to attract someone? What style suits you or someone else best? How you *RE*act, *RE*ceive love, what appeals to your aesthetic sense, your tastes? Look no further than Venus. Venus is like a beautiful languid woman who doesn't actually *do* anything, but makes everyone happy because she is so lovely to look at.

Your Venus placement reveals what you want, what arouses you sexually, what you'd like done to you. You can get plenty of insights from your Venus: why, for instance, you like to make love out of doors, why you can be "talked into things," or why you're attracted to people who appeal to your sympathies instead of confident carefree types. Do you have simple tastes or appreciate the royal treatment? Like Mercury, Venus travels close to the sun, so it is usually within two or three signs of your natal sun sign.

How to Find Your Venus Placement
Look up the year of your birth in the column on the left hand side of the chart on page 72. Then follow the line of that year across the page until you come to the date of your birth or the period of time in which your birth falls. The sign heading that column will be your Venus placement.

For instance, if you were born on September 16,

1952, you would find the year 1952, follow the horizontal line to the dates 9/4–9/27, then note that the heading of the vertical column is Libra. Therefore, your Venus would be in Libra.

It is possible that you may have been born on a day when Venus was changing signs. In that case, look up the sign preceding or following the placement shown to determine if the description feels more like your Venus nature.

Venus in Aries
You're the conqueror, the winner who loves games and contests of all sorts. But when the game's over and you've won the prize, you're anxious to get off and running—on to the "next." The one who appeals to you has to be a bit of a tease, always tempting but never quite letting you take the reins. Someone who gives you a good fight often turns you on. You respond fast and with great heat, then tend to burn out. You may make a commitment to someone who lights your fire, then regret it later. The trick is to keep the fire going. Your tastes are trendy, you love the hottest new thing and being the first in your crowd to try or wear it.

Venus in Taurus
Comfort and physical pleasure in all its forms excites you. You respond to tactile, olfactory, visual, audio and taste sensations. Also a sense of leisure and security where you can relax and take your time. Your tastes are basically conservative and classic. You don't want your boat rocked by something that's not tried and true. You find order and predictability comforting and you enjoy people and settings that are substantial as well as beautiful.

Venus in Gemini
You're a great flirt, turned on by the mind first. You

bore easily and often have several jobs, love affairs and activities going on at once so you can switch around. Because you are basically restless, you want the freedom to explore your many interests. And you want a constant flow of people in your life offering new ideas and good, light conversation. Nothing heavy, please. This constant activity can make your life chaotic. Yet you have the ability to bounce back from any complications your multiple-choice existence causes.

Venus in Cancer

Security, security and more security is what this placement demands. You are attracted to domesticity, to having a home to shelter your loved ones. You like romantic, emotional people who can mother you or protect you or whom *you* can mother or protect. You are also attracted to the secretive side of life: illicit love affairs, mysticism, the occult, psychology. You may at some time lead a secret, double life. You may also be a night owl. You are thin-skinned and can't take *any* criticism; you respond to people who support you, make you feel comfortable and stable. The problem here is that you also have a negative perverse streak that sets yourself up to be victimized. You may actually be attracted to the meanies—a tendency to watch.

Venus in Leo

You like the royal treatment, first class all the way. You're naturally dramatic and quite capable of creating a scene to get your fair—or unfair—share of attention. Flattery and applause get you every time. Pride could be your downfall in love. You're not about to make an effort to win someone over. You love to be waited on, and you love people who look like a million around you, with lots of jewelry, preferably real gold. And if they're your audience, constantly giving you adulation and adoration, so much the better!

Venus in Virgo

You're Mr. or Ms. Clean. Everything has to be in order and spotless. Yet underneath there might be a few naughty fantasies. You see lovemaking as a healthy workout. Men with this placement want their women in white, cooking health foods, but wearing sexy underwear. Women tend to love rather cool workaholics, who won't interfere with their activities. You like to remodel and makeover people and places. Not one to sit still for long, you must be doing something worthwhile to feel good.

Venus in Libra

Peace, beauty, harmony and justice win you over. You want a tranquil atmosphere, gracious living, everything balanced and well-ordered. You like pretty people, good conversation, and a loving partner to share life with. You may be a bit indolent, reluctant to pursue anything that might require a struggle, being in a disagreeable atmosphere or performing an unpleasant chore. You like to analyze problems but may have difficulty making final decisions if this placement is strong. It may be necessary to search for a much more opinionated, decisive partner. Watch a tendency to inaction, laziness. You may be too *re*active for your own good.

Venus in Scorpio

You like 'em hard to get! You're attracted to people who leave you guessing and don't show their hand. You may also like power struggles with those who don't give in easily. Wishy-washy people, bland colors or surroundings that are too calm and peaceful are not for you. Dark or intense colors, all-or-nothing temperaments and heavy wood furniture have the right appeal. You're not afraid of drama and can create quite a scene, especially when it involves going to emotional extremes with the opposite sex. You like mysteries,

crime, the occult and psychic pursuits. You're possessive of everything and everybody—a very jealous type.

Venus in Sagittarius
You love the great outdoors and wide-open spaces.
This is a Venus with wanderlust and a love of adventure. You're happiest when on the move, with an energetic, fun-loving companion—or several. You're a
philosopher who prefers romance to commitment. Lovemaking for you is an active sport, to be enjoyed with a
sense of humor. You get more serious about religion or
philosophy, or your favorite pet. Chances are, it's a big
dog or a horse. You're the great equestrian of the
zodiac.

Venus in Capricorn
You like someone you can introduce to your mother, a
traditional type who won't do anything crazy, who will
support you in a solid substantial way and present a
conservative image. You may fantasize about the opposite type just for fun, but you'd never take them seriously. Besides, you'd rather not waste time on frivolities.
Better to get down to business. You like serious activities, directed toward accomplishments. You may also be
attracted to older people, antique furniture and fine
old mansions.

Venus in Aquarius
You may have a take it or leave it attitude toward love.
It's too sticky. You're more attracted to friendship, to
group activities. You like to have a lot of people around
you and attract people easily. You're also fascinated by
the phenomenon of fame. Or you may choose someone
from a background or race radically different from
yours. You like the unpredictable, the original. You're
not one for the tried and true. Platonic friendship
comes first, then love. You have highly original, often

eccentric tastes that are never governed by what others think or do. You enjoy mental pursuits, discovering something new.

Venus in Pisces
This is considered the best placement for Venus, yet it is much-maligned for its self-sacrificing tendencies. You're attracted to those who demand you give of yourself. You tend to fall for sob stories and adopt stray animals and people. Or you may be attracted to someone who is handicapped physically or emotionally. You often attract hangers-on who take advantage of you. You love to make others happy, to feel you have truly helped. You also love romance and fantasy and may see your beloved through rose-colored glasses.

Mars—The Macho Planet
That Gets You Moving

Mars is what you do to people. How you manipulate, maneuver, drive them crazy, make love to them. Mars is your energy—or lack of it. Some Mars placements are dynamic, movers and shakers. Others operate on a more subliminal level. Some move slowly and deliberately; others are hyper: everywhere—with everybody—at once.

Mars also shows how you get rid of your energy and anger; it determines whether you blow off steam or quietly seethe, express hostility by nagging and fault-finding or by escaping on the next plane to the Bahamas or to the nearest pub. Or is your Mars an expert at giving the silent treatment. It's handy to know your Mars and those of your closest associates. That's their boiling point, their last straw. But unlike your Venus or Mercury, your Mars can be found in any sign of the zodiac.

How to Find Your Mars Placement

To find your Mars influence on the chart on page 78, look up the year of your birth in the left column, then follow the line across horizontally until you come to the column headed by the month of your birth. There you will find an abbreviation of your Mars sign.

If the description of your Mars sign doesn't seem to ring true for you, read the descriptions of the signs preceding and following yours. It is possible that you were born on a day when the planet was changing signs, so your Mars may be in the adjacent sign.

Mars in Aries

This is a super-hot Mars that gives you great energy and drive and a very short fuse. You hate to wait a minute for anything. In your haste to get up and at 'em, you may not look where you're going, or consider the effect of that exciting activity on others. When someone squelches your enthusiasm, you are as crestfallen as a child, yet you'll find a new person or project soon and pursue it with equal vigor. You have a hot temper and life's circumstances may force you to control it and to learn patience.

Mars in Taurus

This Mars gives you perseverance and staying power. Once your energies are engaged, you never give up, but stay right on course. "Stubborn" is your middle name. You're a slow burner, but you can be tyrannical and domineering; you like to control and "own" others and have little tolerance for insubordination. But you can build and accomplish much. You get solid results and go for long-term goals rather than flash-in-the-pan schemes.

Mars in Gemini

Variety is everything to you. You're restless and "antsy."

Always looking for greener pastures. You bore easily; it's very hard to stick to things, jobs or people. You are best off with a lot of telephone lines, at least two jobs at once and perhaps two loves. (This placement is not known for fidelity). You have good coordination, an ability to do things with your hands as well as mental and verbal dexterity.

Mars in Cancer

Mars in Cancer demands and will fight for privacy, comfort, a secure home. You are easily threatened and risks make you irritable and emotionally upset (and you are very prone to stomach troubles). Yet you can shrewdly assess others' weaknesses and play on them if need be. You are very intuitive in your actions and can sense what others need, which makes you a terrific lover. But you rarely confront others directly, you take a roundabout approach that may seem sneaky to others, while you are actually camouflaging your feelings to protect your vulnerability.

Mars in Leo

A powerful placement that gives you great drama and presence. You're almost too hot to handle. You do things in a big way or not at all. You love being the best at whatever you do, and making sure others know it. You naturally head for a position of authority where you can direct others. You have a flair for spectacle and head right for center stage. You are physically strong and vital, love to gamble for high stakes but should avoid taking physical risks. You love to lavish your lover with the best of everything and display affection with great warmth. Some people may find you a bit overwhelming.

Mars in Virgo

This is a very fussy Mars with definite likes and dislikes. But you are very hardworking. In fact, you tend to work at everything (no one can do the job as well as you). You are super critical of others and tend to nag when they don't live up to your standards. Put your ability to good use organizing others, designing practical things and communicating by "teaching" rather than faultfinding. Under pressure, you get irritable and hyper and could suffer from stomach trouble. Sexually, you like to serve your lover, once you've found the "perfect" one and only.

Mars in Libra

You'll go for looks every time. And you love to be belle of the ball, surrounded by attractive and adoring members of the opposite sex. You are always looking for the perfect partner and find it difficult to decide on any one person. You have a very active, refined mind and you love to debate—rarely losing your cool, except when there is blatant injustice. You act out your anger by throwing others off-balance, or by infuriating them with your indecision. But, more often, you charm people into doing what you want and often get away with murder. You work to create beauty and harmony; you would make a great designer or lawyer.

Mars in Scorpio

This is a tough, driving Mars that works relentlessly to achieve goals. You're not afraid of dirty work. You push yourself longer and harder than anyone! And you don't give up. You do everything intensely and woe betide the person who crosses you. You will attack relentlessly until you get revenge. You are a jealous possessive type, with one of the zodiac's strongest sex drives and very definite likes and dislikes. You are a great problem solver, digging beneath the surface until you get the best answers. Everything you do is done with a purpose, to get results. You're a great manipula-

tor, using others' energy to further your own goals.
Your temper can be violent or at least sarcastic and cuts
deep! (This is a great placement for a surgeon.)

Mars in Sagittarius

Always on the move, you're a natural athlete with a
carefree, independent outlook. You are very impulsive
and will speak your mind, unafraid of the consequences
and pack up and leave at a moment's notice. Lovemaking for you is a great aerobic exercise, not to be taken
too seriously. You're liable to crack a joke at any time.
Your good-natured attitude spills over into work, where
you are well liked but may not always be responsible.
You are too busy looking at the big picture to worry
about the vital details. When angry, you'll tell everyone
off in no uncertain terms, with little regard for the
consequences. You're a big gambler, often leaving everything to chance.

Mars in Capricorn

A very hard-working achiever, you're a good organizer
with a strong drive to get ahead. You'll often use
people—including lovers—to advance your goals. You
pursue the influential and the powerful, making carefully calculated steps up the ladder. You tend to bury
your real feelings under a cool facade, but will take
definite action when provoked. You like to be in control and often take on too much responsibility so others
will depend on you. You may also go for much older or
younger lovers—odd age gaps.

Mars in Aquarius

There's safety in numbers, you believe. It's hard to get
close to you as you're always surrounded by people.
Intimacy is not your strong point. You often experiment with love but keep emotions at a distance. You
are best off when you pursue a lofty goal and a partner

who is also a friend. You surprise people and like to shock them sometimes. You enjoy breaking rules, sometimes for the sheer fun of it. You occasionally act contrary just to shake people up. Your eccentricity and unpredictability can turn potential lovers off.

Mars in Pisces

A great placement for a film actor or for any job where you have to create illusion or play roles. You may have a problem with reality, however; it's just not romantic and glamorous enough. You let out your aggressions through emotional manipulation, playing helpless, misunderstood or vulnerable to get your way. You are a master martyr. Chances are, your lover plays a caretaker role in your life. You have a great desire to help the underdog and are kind to the less fortunate and supportive of your friends. As a lover, you are affectionate, unselfish and sensitive; you enjoy pleasing others.

VENUS SIGN 1910–1975

	Aries	Taurus	Gemini	Cancer	Leo	Virgo
1910	5/7-6/3	6/4-6/29	6/30-7/24	7/25-8/18	8/19-9/12	9/13-10/6
1911	2/28-3/23	3/24-4/17	4/18-5/12	5/13-6/8	6/9-7/7	7/8-11/8
1912	4/13-5/6	5/7-5/31	6/1-6/24	6/24-7/18	7/19-8/12	8/13-9/5
1913	2/3-3/6	3/7-5/1	7/8-8/5	8/6-8/31	9/1-9/26	9/27-10/20
	5/2-5/30	5/31-7/7				
1914	3/14-4/6	4/7-5/1	5/2-5/25	5/26-6/19	6/20-7/15	7/16-8/10
1915	4/27-5/21	5/22-6/15	6/16-7/10	7/11-8/3	8/4-8/28	8/29-9/21
1916	2/14-3/9	3/10-4/5	4/6-5/5	5/6-9/8	9/9-10/7	10/8-11/2
1917	3/29-4/21	4/22-5/15	5/16-6/9	6/10-7/3	7/4-7/28	7/29-8/21
1918	5/7-6/2	6/3-6/28	6/29-7/24	7/25-8/18	8/19-9/11	9/12-10/5
1919	2/27-3/22	3/23-4/16	4/17-5/12	5/13-6/7	6/8-7/7	7/8-11/8
1920	4/12-5/6	5/7-5/30	5/31-6/23	6/24-7/18	7/19-8/11	8/12-9/4
1921	2/3-3/6	3/7-4/25	7/8-8/5	8/6-8/31	9/1-9/25	9/26-10/20
	4/26-6/1	6/2-7/7				
1922	3/13-4/6	4/7-4/30	5/1-5/25	5/26-6/19	6/20-7/14	7/15-8/9
1923	4/27-5/21	5/22-6/14	6/15-7/9	7/10-8/3	8/4-8/27	8/28-9/20
1924	2/13-3/8	3/9-4/4	4/5-5/5	5/6-9/8	9/9-10/7	10/8-11/12
1925	3/28-4/20	4/21-5/15	5/16-6/8	6/9-7/3	7/4-7/27	7/28-8/21
1926	5/7-6/2	6/3-6/28	6/29-7/23	7/24-8/17	8/18-9/11	9/12-10/5
1927	2/27-3/22	3/23-4/16	4/17-5/11	5/12-6/7	6/8-7/7	7/8-11/9
1928	4/12-5/5	5/6-5/29	5/30-6/23	6/24-7/17	7/18-8/11	8/12-9/4
1929	2/3-3/7	3/8-4/19	7/8-8/4	8/5-8/30	8/31-9/25	9/26-10/19
	4/20-6/2	6/3-7/7				
1930	3/13-4/5	4/6-4/30	5/1-5/24	5/25-6/18	6/19-7/14	7/15-8/9
1931	4/26-5/20	5/21-6/13	6/14-7/8	7/9-8/2	8/3-8/26	8/27-9/19

VENUS SIGN 1910–1975

Libra	Scorpio	Sagittarius	Capricorn	Aquarius	Pisces
10/7-10/30	10/31-11/23	11/24-12/17	12/18-12/31	1/1-1/15	1/16-1/28
				1/29-4/4	4/5-5/6
11/19-12/8	12/9-12/31		1/1-1/10	1/11-2/2	2/3-2/27
9/6-9/30	1/1-1/4	1/5-1/29	1/30-2/23	2/24-3/18	3/19-4/12
	10/1-10/24	10/25-11/17	11/18-12/12	12/13-12/31	
10/21-11/13	11/14-12/7	12/8-12/31		1/1-1/6	1/7-2/2
8/11-9/6	9/7-10/9	10/10-12/5	1/1-1/24	1/25-2/17	2/18-3/13
	12-6/12-30	12/31			
9/22-10/15	10/16-11/8	1/1-2/6	2/7-3/6	3/7-4/1	4/2-4/26
		11/9-12/2	12/3-12/26	12/27-12/31	
11/3-11/27	11/28-12/21	12/22-12/31		1/1-1/19	1/20-2/13
8/22-9/16	9/17-10/11	1/1-1/14	1/15-2/7	2/8-3/4	3/5-3/28
		10/12-11/6	11/7-12/5	12/6-12/31	
10/6-10/29	10/30-11/22	11/23-12/16	12/17-12/31	1/1-4/5	4/6-5/6
11/9-12/8	12/9-12/31		1/1-1/9	1/10-2/2	2/3-2/26
9/5-9/30	1/1-1/3	1/4-1/28	1/29-2/22	2/23-3/18	3/19-4/11
	9/31-10/23	10/24-11/17	11/18-12/11	12/12-12/31	
10/21-11/13	11/14-12/7	12/8-12/31		1/1-1/6	1/7-2/2
8/10-9/6	9/7-10/10	10/11-11/28	1/1-1/24	1/25-2/16	2/17-3/12
	11/29-12/31				
9/21-10/14	1/1	1/2-2/6	2/7-3/5	3/6-3/31	4/1-4/26
	10/15-11/7	11/8-12/1	12/2-12/25	12/26-12/31	
11/3-11/26	11/27-12/21	12/22-12/31		1/1-1/19	1/20-2/12
8/22-9/15	9/16-10/11	1/1-1/14	1/15-2/7	2/8-3/3	3/4-3/27
		10/12-11/6	11/7-12/5	12/6-12/31	
10/6-10/29	10/30-11/22	11/23-12/16	12/17-12/31	1/1-4/5	4/6-5/6
11/10-12/8	12/9-12/31	1/1-1/7	1/8	1/9-2/1	2/2-2/26
9/5-9/28	1/1-1/3	1/4-1/28	1/29-2/22	2/23-3/17	3/18-4/11
	9/29-10/23	10/24-11/16	11/17-12/11	12/12-12/31	
10/20-11/12	11/13-12/6	12/7-12/30	12/31	1/1-1/5	1/6-2/2
8/10-9/6	9/7-10/11	10/12-11/21	1/1-1/23	1/24-2/16	2/17-3/12
	11/22-12/31				
9/20-10/13	1/1-1/3	1/4-2/6	2/7-3/4	3/5-3/31	4/1-4/25
	10/14-11/6	11/7-11/30	12/1-12/24	12/25-12/31	

VENUS SIGN 1910–1975

	Aries	Taurus	Gemini	Cancer	Leo	Virgo
1932	2/12-3/8	3/9-4/3	4/4-5/5 7/13-7/27	5/6-7/12 7/28-9/8	9/9-10/6	10/7-11/1
1933	3/27-4/19	4/20-5/28	5/29-6/8	6/9-7/2	7/3-7/26	7/27-8/20
1934	5/6-6/1	6/2-6/27	6/28-7/22	7/23-8/16	8/17-9/10	9/11-10/4
1935	2/26-3/21	3/22-4/15	4/16-5/10	5/11-6/6	6/7-7/6	7/7-11/8
1936	4/11-5/4	5/5-5/28	5/29-6/22	6/23-7/16	7/17-8/10	8/11-9/4
1937	2/2-3/8 4/14-6/3	3/9-4/17 6/4-7/6	7/7-8/3	8/4-8/29	8/30-9/24	9/25-10/18
1938	3/12-4/4	4/5-4/28	4/29-5/23	5/24-6/18	6/19-7/13	7/14-8/8
1939	4-25/5/19	5/20-6/13	6/14-7/8	7/9-8/1	8/2-8/25	8/26-9/19
1940	2/12-3/7	3/8-4/3	4/4-5/5 7/5-7/31	5/6-7/4 8/1-9/8	9/9-10/5	10/6-10/31
1941	3/27-4/19	4/20-5/13	5/14-6/6	6/7-6/1	7/2-7/26	7/27-8/20
1942	5/6-6/1	6/2-6/26	6/27-7/22	7/23-8/16	8/17-9/9	9/10-10/3
1943	2/25-3/20	3/21-4/14	4/15-5/10	5/11-6/6	6/7-7/6	7/7-11/8
1944	4-10/5-3	5/4-5/28	5/29-6/21	6/22-7/16	7/17-8/9	8/10-9/2
1945	2/2-3/10 4/7-6/3	3/11-4/6 6/4-7/6	7/7-8/3	8/4-8/29	8/30-9/23	9/24-10/18
1946	3/11-4/4	4/5-4/28	4/29-5/23	5/24-6/17	6/18-7/12	7/13-8/8
1947	4/25-5/19	5/20-6/12	6/13-7/7	7/8-8/1	8/2-8/25	8/26-9/18
1948	2/11-3/7	3/8-4/3	4/4-5/6 6/29-8/2	5/7-6/28 8/3-9/7	9/8-10/5	10/6-10/31
1949	3/26-4/19	4/20-5/13	5/14-6/6	6/7-6/30	7/1-7/25	7/26-8/19
1950	5/5-5/31	6/1-6/26	6/27-7/21	7/22-8/15	8/16-9/9	9/10-10/3
1951	2/25-3/21	3/22-4/15	4/16-5/10	5/11-6/6	6/7-7/7	7/8-11/9
1952	4/10-5/4	5/5-5/28	5/29-6/21	6/22-7/16	7/17-8/9	8/10-9/3
1953	2/2-3/13 4/1-6/5	3/4-3/31 6/6-7/7	7/8-8/3	8/4-8/29	8/30-9/24	9/25-10/18

Libra	Scorpio	Sagittarius	Capricorn	Aquarius	Pisces
11/2-11/25	11/26-12/20	12/21-12/31		1/1-1/18	1/19-2/11
8/21-9/14	9/15-10/10	1/1-1/13	1/14-2/6	2/7-3/2	3/3-3/26
		10/11-11/5	11/6-12/4	12/5-12/31	
10/5-10/28	10/29-11/21	11/22-12/15	12/16-12/31	1/1-4/5	4/6-5/5
11/9-12/7	12/8-12/31		1/1-1/7	1/8-1/31	2/1-2/25
9/5-9/27	1/1-1/2	1/3-1/27	1/28-2/21	2/22-3/16	3/17-4/10
	9/28-10/22	10/23-11/15	11/16-12/10	12/11-12/31	
10/19-11/11	11/12-12/5	12/6-12/29	12/30-12/31	1/1-1/5	1/6-2/1
8/9-9/6	9/7-10/13	10/14-11/14	1/1-1/22	1/23-2/15	2/16-3/11
	11/15-12/31				
9/20-10/13	1/1-1/3	1/4-2/5	2/6-3/4	3/5-3/30	3/31-4/24
	10/14-11/6	11/7-11/30	12/1-12/24	12/25-12/31	
11/1-11/25	11/26-12/19	12/20-12/31		1/1-1/18	1/19-2/11
8/21-9/14	9/15-10/9	1/1-1/12	1/13-2/5	2/6-3/1	3/2-3/26
		10/10-11/5	11/6-12/4	12/5-12/31	
10/4-10/27	10/28-11/20	11/21-12/14	12/15-12/31	1/1-4/4	4/6-5/5
11/9-12/7	12/8-12/31		1/1-1/7	1/8-1/31	2/1-2/24
9/3-9/27	1/1-1/2	1/3-1/27	1/28-2/20	2/21-3/16	3/17-4/9
	9/28-10/21	10/22-11/15	11/16-12/10	12/11-12/31	
10/19-11/11	11/12-12/5	12/6-12/29	12/30-12/31	1/1-1/4	1/5-2/1
8/9-9/6	9/7-10/15	10/16-11/7	1/1-1/21	1/22-2/14	2/15-3/10
	11/8-12/31				
9/19-10/12	1/1-1/4	1/5-2/5	2/6-3/4	3/5-3/29	3/30-4/24
	10/13-11/5	11/6-11/29	11/30-12/23	12/24-12/31	
11/1-1/25	11/26-12/19	12/20-12/31		1/1-1/17	1/18-2/10
8/20-9/14	9/15-10/9	1/1-1/12	1/13-2/5	2/6-3/1	3/2-3/25
		10/10-11/5	11/6-12/5	12/6-12/31	
10/4-10/27	10/28-11/20	11/21-12/13	12/14-12/31	1/1-4/5	4/6-5/4
11/10-12/7	12/8-12/31		1/1-1/7	1/8-1/31	2/1-2/24
9/4-9/27	1/1-1/2	1/3-1/27	1/28-2/20	2/21-3/16	3/17-4/9
	9/28-10/21	10/22-11/15	11/16-12/10	12/11-12/31	
10/19-11/11	11/12-12/5	12/6-12/29	12/30-12/31	1/1-1/5	1/6-2/1

VENUS SIGN 1910–1975

	Aries	Taurus	Gemini	Cancer	Leo	Virgo
1954	3/12-4/4	4/5-4/28	4/29-5/23	5/24-6/17	6/18-7/13	7/14-8/8
1955	4/25-5/19	5/20-6/13	6/14-7/7	7/8-8/1	8/2-8/25	8/26-9/18
1956	2/12-3/7	3/8-4/4	4/5-5/7 6:24-8/4	5/8-6/23 8/5-9/8	9/9-10/5	10/6-10/31
1957	3-26/4-19	4/20-5/13	5/14-6/6	6/7-7/1	7/2-7/26	7/27-8/19
1958	5-6/5-31	6/1-6/26	6/27-7/22	7/23-8/15	8/16-9/9	9/10-10/3
1959	2-25/3-20	3/21-4/14	4/15-5/10	5/11-6/6	6/7-7/8 9/21-9/24	7/9-9/20 9/25-11/9
1960	4-10/5-3	5/4-5/28	5/29-6/21	6/22-7/15	7/16-8/9	8/10-9/2
1961	2-3/6-5	6/6-7/7	7/8-8/3	8/4-8/29	8/30-9/23	9/24-10/17
1962	3/11-4/3	4/4-4/28	4/29-5/22	5/23-6/17	6/18-7/12	7/13-8/8
1963	4/24-5/18	5/19-6/12	6/13-7/7	7/8-7/31	8/1-8/25	8/26-9/18
1964	2/11-3/7	3/8-4/4	4/5-5/9 6/18-8/5	5/10-6/17 8/6-9/8	9/9-10/5	10/6-10/31
1965	3/26-4/18	4/19-5/12	5/13-6/6	6/7-6/30	7/1-7/25	7/26-8/19
1966	5/6-6/31	6/1-6/26	6/27-7/21	7/22-8/15	8/16-9/8	9/9-10/2
1967	2/24-3/20	3/21-4/14	4/15-5/10	5/11-6/6	6/7-7/8 9/10-10/1	7/9-9/9 10/2-11/9
1968	4/9-5/3	5/4-5/27	5/28-6/20	6/21-7/15	7/16-8/8	8/9-9/2
1969	2/3-6/6	6/7-7/6	7/7-8/3	8/4-8/28	8/29-9/22	9/23-10/17
1970	3/11-4/3	4/4-4/27	4/28-5/22	5/23-6/16	6/17-7/12	7/13-8/8
1971	4/24-5/18	5/19-6/12	6/13-7/6	7/7-7/31	8/1-8/24	8/25-9/17
1972	2/11-3/7	3/8-4/3	4/4-5/10 6/12-8/6	5/11-6/11 8/7-9/8	9/9-10/5	10/6-10/30
1973	3/25-4/18	4/18-5/12	5/13-6/5	6/6-6/29	7/1-7/25	7/26-8/19
1974	5/5-5/31	6/1-6/25	6/26-7/21	7/22-8/14	8/15-9/8	9/9-10/2
1975	2/24-3/20	3/21-4/13	4/14-5/9	5/10-6/6	6/7-7/9 9/3-10/4	7/10-9/2 10/5-11/9

VENUS SIGN 1910–1975

Libra	Scorpio	Sagittarius	Capricorn	Aquarius	Pisces
8/9-9/6	9/7-10/22	10/23-10/27	1/1-1/22	1/23-2/15	2/16-3/11
	10/28-12/31				
9/19-10/13	1/1-1/6	1/7-2/5	2/6-3/4	3/5-3/30	3/31-4/24
	10/14-11/5	11/6-11/30	12/1-12/24	12/25-12/31	
11/1-11/25	11/26-12/19	12/20-12/31		1/1-1/17	1/18-2/11
8/20-9/14	9/15-10/9	1/1-1/12	1/13-2/5	2/6-3/1	3/2-3/25
		10/10-11/5	11/6-12/16	12/7-12/31	
10/4-10/27	10/28-11/20	11/21-12/14	12/15-12/31	1/1-4/6	4/7-5/5
11/10-12/7	12/8-12/31		1/1-1/7	1/8-1/31	2/1-2/24
9/3-9/26	1/1-1/2	1/3-1/27	1/28-2/20	2/21-3/15	3/16-4/9
	9/27-10/21	10/22-11/15	11/16-12/10	12/11-12/31	
10/18-11/11	11/12-12/4	12/5-12/28	12/29-12/31	1/1-1/5	1/6-2/2
8/9-9/6	9/7-12/31		1/1-1/21	1/22-2/14	2/15-3/10
9/19-10/12	1/1-1/6	1/7-2/5	2/6-3/4	3/5-3/29	3/30-4/23
	10/13-11/5	11/6-11/29	11/30-12/23	12/24-12/31	
11/1-11/24	11/25-12/19	12/20-12/31		1/1-1/16	1/17-2/10
8/20-9/13	9/14-10/9	1/1-1/12	1/13-2/5	2/6-3/1	3/2-3/25
		10/10-11/5	11/6-12/7	12/8-12/31	
10/3-10/26	10/27-11/19	11/20-12/13	2/7-2/25	1/1-2/6	4/7-5/5
			12/14-12/31	2/26-4/6	
11/10-12/7	12/8-12/23		1/1-1/6	1/7-1/30	1/31-2/23
9/3-9/26	1/1	1/2-1/26	1/27-2/20	2/21-3/15	3/16-4/8
	9/27-10/21	10/22-11/14	11/15-12/9	12/10-12/31	
10/18-11/10	11/11-12/4	12/5-12/28	12/29-12/31	1/1-1/4	1/5-2/2
8/9-9/7	9/8-12/31		1/1-1/21	1/22-2/14	2/15-3/10
9/18-10/11	1/1-1/7	1/8-2/5	2/6-3/4	3/5-3/29	3/30-4/23
	10/12-11/5	11/6-11/29	11/30-12/23	12/24-12/31	
	11/25-12/18	12/19-12/31		1/1-1/16	1/17-2/10
10/31-11/24					
8/20-9/13		1/1-1/12	1/13-2/4	2/5-2/28	3/1-3/24
		10/9-11/5	11/6-12/7	12/8-12/31	
			1/30-2/28	1/1-1/29	
10/3-10/26	10/27-11/19	11/20-12/13	12/14-12/31	3/1-4/6	4/7-5/4
			1/1-1/6	1/7-1/30	1/31-2/23
11/10-12/7	12/8-12/31				

MARS SIGN 1910-1975

	Jan.	Feb.	Mar.	Apr.	May	June	July	Aug.	Sept.	Oct.	Nov.	Dec.
1910	AR	TA	GE	GE	CA	CA	LE	VI	VI	LI	SC	SC
1911	SA	CP	AQ	AQ	PI	AR	TA	TA	GE	GE	GE	TA
1912	TA	GE	GE	CA	CA	LE	LE	VI	LI	LI	SC	SA
1913	CP	CP	AQ	PI	AR	AR	TA	GE	CA	CA	CA	CA
1914	CA	CA	CA	CA	LE	LE	VI	LI	LI	SC	SA	SA
1915	CP	AQ	PI	PI	AR	TA	GE	LI	CA	LE	LE	LE
1916	LE	LE	LE	LE	LE	VI	VI	LI	SC	SC	SA	CP
1917	AQ	AQ	PI	AR	TA	GE	GE	CA	LE	LE	VI	VI
1918	LI	LI	VI	VI	VI	VI	LI	LI	SC	SA	CP	CP
1919	AQ	PI	AR	TA	GE	CA	CA	LE	VI	VI	CP	LI
1920	LI	SC	SC	SC	LI	LI	SC	SC	SA	SA	VI	AQ
1921	PI	AR	AR	TA	GE	GE	CA	LE	LE	VI	CP	LI
1922	SC	SC	SA	SA	SA	GE	SA	SA	CP	CP	LI	AQ
1923	PI	AR	TA	TA	GE	CA	CA	LE	VI	VI	AQ	SC
1924	SC	SA	CP	CP	AQ	AQ	PI	PI	AQ	AQ	LI	PI
1925	AR	TA	TA	GE	CA	CA	LE	VI	VI	LI	PI	SC
1926	SA	CP	CP	AQ	PI	AQ	AR	VI	VI	TA	SC	TA
1927	TA	TA	GE	GE	CA	LE	LE	VI	LI	LI	TA	SA
1928	SA	SA	AQ	PI	PI	AR	TA	GE	GE	CA	CA	CA

	Jan.	Feb.	Mar.	Apr.	May	June	July	Aug.	Sept.	Oct.	Nov.	Dec.
1929	GE	GE	CA	CA	LE	LE	VI	VI	LI	SC	SC	SA
1930	CP	AQ	AQ	PI	AR	TA	GE	GE	CA	CA	LE	LE
1931	LE	LE	CA	LE	LE	VI	VI	LI	LI	SC	SA	CP
1932	CP	AQ	PI	AR	TA	TA	GE	CA	CA	LE	VI	VI
1933	VI	VI	VI	VI	VI	VI	LI	LI	SC	SA	SA	CP
1934	AQ	PI	AR	AR	TA	GE	GE	CA	LE	LE	VI	LI
1935	LI	LI	LI	LI	LI	LI	LI	SC	SC	SA	CP	AQ
1936	PI	PI	AR	TA	GE	GE	CA	LE	LE	VI	LI	LI
1937	SC	SC	SA	SA	SC	SC	SC	SA	SA	CP	AQ	AQ
1938	PI	AR	TA	TA	GE	CA	CA	LE	VI	VI	LI	SC
1939	SC	SA	SA	CP	CP	AQ	AQ	CP	CP	AQ	AQ	PI
1940	AR	AR	TA	GE	GE	CA	LE	LE	VI	VI	LI	SC
1941	SA	SA	CP	AQ	AQ	PI	AR	AR	AR	AR	AR	AR
1942	TA	TA	GE	GE	CA	LE	LE	VI	VI	LI	SC	SC
1943	SA	CP	AQ	AQ	PI	AR	TA	TA	GE	GE	GE	GE
1944	GE	GE	GE	GE	CA	LE	VI	VI	LI	SC	SC	SA
1945	CP	AQ	AQ	PI	AR	TA	TA	GE	CA	CA	LE	LE
1946	CA	CA	CA	CA	LE	LE	VI	LI	LI	SC	SA	SA
1947	CP	AQ	PI	AR	AR	TA	GE	CA	CA	LE	LE	VI

MARS SIGN 1910-1975

	Jan.	Feb.	Mar.	Apr.	May	June	July	Aug.	Sept.	Oct.	Nov.	Dec.
1948	VI	LE	LE	LE	LE	VI	VI	LI	SC	SC	SA	CP
1949	AQ	PI	PI	AR	TA	GE	GE	CA	LE	LE	VI	VI
1950	LI	LI	LI	VI	VI	LI	LI	SC	SC.	SA	CP	CP
1951	AQ	PI	AR	TA	TA	GE	CA	CA	LE	VI	VI	LI
1952	LI	SC	SC	SC	SC	SC	SC	SC	SA	CP	CP	LI
1953	AR	AR	AR	TA	GE	GE	CA	LE	VI	VI	LI	AQ
1954	SC	SA	SA	CP	CP	CP	SA	SA	CP	CP	AQ	LI
1955	PI	AR	TA	GE	GE	CA	LE	LE	VI	LI	LI	PI
1956	SA	SA	CP	AQ	AQ	PI	PI	PI	PI	PI	PI	SC
1957	AR	TA	TA	GE	CA	CA	AR	VI	VI	LI	SC	AR
1958	SA	CP	CP	AQ	PI	AR	LE	TA	TA	GE	TA	SC
1959	TA	GE	GE	CA	CA	LE	LE	VI	LI	LI	SC	TA
1960	CP	CP	AQ	CA	AR	AR	TA	GE	GE	CA	CA	SA
1961	CA	CA	CA	CA	LE	TA	VI	VI	LI	SC	SA	CA
1962	CP	AQ	PI	PI	PI	TA	GE	GE	CA	LE	SA	SA
1963	LE	LE	LE	LE	LE	TA	VI	LI	SC	SC	LE	CP
1964	AQ	AQ	AR	AR	TA	VI	GE	CA	LE	LE	SA	CA
1965	VI	VI	VI	VI	VI	VI	LI	LI	SC	SA	VI	CP
1966	AQ	PI	AR	AR	TA	GE	CA	CA	LE	VI	VI	LI

MARS SIGN 1918–1975

	Jan.	Feb.	Mar.	Apr.	May	June	July	Aug.	Sept.	Oct.	Nov.	Dec.
1967	LI	SC	SC	LI	LI	LI	LI	SC	SA	SA	CP	AQ
1968	PI	PI	AR	TA	GE	GE	CA	LE	LE	VI	LI	LI
1969	SC	SC	SA	SA	SA	SA	SA	SA	SA	CP	AQ	PI
1970	PI	AR	TA	TA	GE	CA	CA	LE	VI	VI	LI	SC
1971	SC	SA	CP	CP	AQ	AQ	AQ	AQ	AQ	AQ	PI	PI
1972	AR	TA	TA	GE	CA	CA	LE	LE	VI	LI	SC	SC
1973	SA	CP	CP	AQ	PI	PI	AR	TA	TA	TA	AR	AR
1974	TA	TA	GE	GE	CA	LE	LE	VI	LI	LI	SC	SA
1975	SA	CP	AQ	PI	PI	AR	TA	GE	GE	GE	CA	GE

AR—Aries　　　　LE—Leo　　　　　SA—Sagittarius
TA—Taurus　　　VI—Virgo　　　　CP—Capricorn
GE—Gemini　　　LI—Libra　　　　AQ—Aquarius
CA—Cancer　　　SC—Scorpio　　　PI—Pisces

6

Saturn and Jupiter:
The Planets of Fate and Fortune

Saturn Offers Challenge

The image of the beautiful planet Saturn, surrounded by layers of rings, can be quite useful to us astrologically if we think of its rings as fences or barriers to be hurdled. Saturn represents those areas of life where we meet obstacles, where we are tested, where we are literally fenced in by life's circumstances. It presents us with challenges we need in order to grow up. As you pass over or through the rings of Saturn, you become wiser, more mature. You develop judgment.

Few of us look forward to a time when we are tested by Saturn, but you can look at it positively as a time when you can make substantial progress by discovering your own weaknesses and eliminating obstacles. It won't be easy, but then growing up never is.

In your lifetime, Saturn will probably move through every sign of the zodiac at least once. It takes 28 to 30 years to complete a Saturn cycle. During that cycle you'll be tested in every area of life. Depending on where Saturn is traveling in your individual horoscope, you'll be forced to shape up (to get organized and acquire discipline) and take stock. Sometimes the experience is painful, but it will be less so if you remember that Saturn's learning and growing experiences are inevitable. Look upon them positively as chances to evaluate who you are and where you're going. Saturn is the price you pay for freedom—your trade-offs in life.

In 1988 Capricorns and Sagittarians will have this planet passing their natal sun sign, which means testing and growing experiences for them in particular. Other signs affected when Saturn is in Capricorn will be Aries, Cancer and Libra. During the times when Saturn swings back into Sagittarius, it will affect Pisces, Gemini and Virgo.

You can get insights into how you take on responsibilities, how you get organized, how you work and where *you* need work by the placement of Saturn at your birth. Check these descriptions for clues, if you don't know your natal Saturn, and for confirmation, if you do!

Saturn in Aries
This is the boss who wants to do everything himself. You must learn to delegate authority and deal with your fear of being pushed around by others.

Saturn in Taurus
You must learn control over material possessions, how to handle money. You may have lean periods, with trouble hanging onto cash.

Saturn in Gemini
He or she learns to listen and concentrate. This is a worrier whose day-to-day communications become learning experiences.

Saturn in Cancer
This person often has to overcome emotional restrictions dating from childhood. One of your parents may

have put you down so badly that you are easily threatened. Your lesson is to build your own nest, your own security. Break away from negative childhood influences.

Saturn in Leo
You tend to be a law unto yourself. It may be difficult for you to cooperate; you want to be boss, the *star*. You resent restrictions and may have a problem dealing with the duties marriage and children impose.

Saturn in Virgo
This combination tends to be its own worst enemy. Obsession with details makes life difficult for everyone. Watch runaway guilt feelings, psychosomatic illnesses. Learn diet and exercise routines to take care of your body.

Saturn in Libra
Here is someone who tests relationships in marriage, business, friendship, legal agreements. Social encounters of all kinds come under scrutiny. You who were born with this placement may delay marriage and need to develop a sense of balance and timing to work in harmony with others.

Saturn in Scorpio
Here is a lonesome soul, afraid of trusting others. Its testing comes through use of power and sex for manipulative purposes. There's often a conflict between giving in to feelings and the need for control at all times.

Saturn in Sagittarius
One can fear being tied down. You'll learn what freedom really means. There's also a fear of outside forces (terrorism) and travel problems. And many challenges to belief systems, a questioning of spiritual values.

Saturn in Capricorn
This is its strongest position, bringing endurance and the dignity of maturity. This is a position where we ask: What will we do to get to the top of our profession or to achieve social or political status? You learn how to use power for long-range benefits.

Saturn in Aquarius
This person shows concern with learning to do for others. Here you deal with peer group pressure. There may be a fear of being different and you're tested by having to deal with the opinion of the world. You worry about what others think.

Saturn in Pisces
This combination brings a fear of isolation and confinement. You learn by giving to others with no thought of personal return and by constantly testing reality vs. illusion.

If Saturn is the finger of fate that points to duty and responsibility, then Jupiter is the open hand of good fortune, the glad hand that pats you on the back.

Jupiter Can Give a Lift—But Be Wary

The physical character of Jupiter also gives us a good reading on the planet. It's the biggest and the brightest member of the sun's family. Yet it is not very substantial. It is made of a swirling mass of gases, more like a big balloon.

Jupiter gives us a lift. It brings abundance (perhaps only temporarily), lucky breaks, a time of expansion and swift movement. When Jupiter is smiling on you, things come more easily, with no work or painful lessons to learn. Unlike Saturn, whose payoffs come from hard work, Jupiter doles out good fortune with an open hand. You're in the right place at the right time; you win the lottery. When squandered, Jupiter becomes lazy, aimless, a drifter and a spendthrift—and fat (Jupiter can expand your waistline by encouraging you to gorge on goodies, or to become pregnant). You have no discipline for diet or exercise, or anything strenuous, for that matter, when Jupiter is in your sun sign.

A good way to take advantage of Jupiter is to go with its higher purposes: expand your mind, travel, try new things. Examine your higher philosophical and religious values, give away money to a worthy cause, start a family! In 1988, Jupiter completes its transit of Aries and enters Taurus on March 9, proceeds briefly in to Gemini on July 22, moves back and forth until December 1, then recedes into Taurus for the remainder of the year. It stays about a year in every sign, so you are in for a windfall every twelve years and a discernable lift when it enters a sign that is especially favorable to your sun sign.

Jupiter in Aries
You take risks on impulse. You're full of self-confidence and enthusiasm, a terrific salesman who is best at selling yourself. Watch out for a tendency to arrogance.

Jupiter in Taurus
This combination brings expensive tastes, no matter what the budget. You need luxury in life and are prone to spend beyond your means. You're often lucky speculating in real estate. Watch for overweight!

Jupiter in Gemini
A love of talk, gossip and constant motion is characteristic. You are very curious and forever studying, especially short school courses. You are a good teacher, too. Foreign languages and writing may come easily to you.

Earn your fortune through communications-related jobs, selling, using your hands.

Jupiter in Cancer
One of the best places for this planet. Food, money and antiques are potential money-makers for you. So is anything to do with caring for children or designing, constructing and decorating houses or shelters. Think of food, shelter, boats and shipping, nursing and politics when it comes to luck. You can really make people feel at home. But watch a tendency to overindulge in food and drink.

Jupiter in Leo
You're expansive and expensive, young at heart, playful and romantic. In fact, you tend to play around a lot. You like to take chances with love and money. You're a terrific charmer, thanks to your positive attitude and flair for the dramatic. Gold, fashion, and the entertainment industry are lucky for you; so are things to do with children's play activities. Lady luck is also with you in gambling or speculative ventures.

Jupiter in Virgo
You expend so much energy on the job, and you work with such a sense of pleasure that you're sure to rise to the top. Others feel you can handle the toughest tasks and keep piling them on, so watch out for overwork. Your expansion is based on sound practical reasoning and good planning rather than speculation. Medicine, publishing (especially editorial or critical work) come easily to you.

Jupiter in Libra
You're the great lawyer or judge who embodies the spirit of fair play. Your luck lies in work with an artistic or humanistic value, where you can express your social

conscience and your good judgment in a harmonious atmosphere. Friends and partners are lucky for you and often bring you money and social position. This position usually brings a happy partnership or marriage.

Jupiter in Scorpio

This Jupiter loves excesses in anything. You can go to extremes in business, sex, wielding of power of any kind. You love powerful cars, mechanical equipment. You seem to have a sixth sense about where the power and money-making opportunities lie and when to pounce. Mysteries, secrets and confidences often figure in your life. You may gravitate to police work, psychiatry, religious cults. Watch out for overindulgence in drugs or alcohol.

Jupiter in Sagittarius

Bighearted and generous, you're always willing to help someone in need. Chances are you travel widely and frequently and hate feeling restricted. Education and jobs related to learning are lucky for you. So are publishing, travel and animals, particularly horses. You have a strong code of honor about everything you do. Look for good fortune in a foreign country.

Jupiter in Capricorn

In this sign of caution and deliberation, expansive Jupiter is restrained. But you will spend if your status, reputation or image is involved. You're very concerned about what others think. You'll spend to connect with the right people, make a deal, sell your project. You're the great wheeler-dealer and lucky in leadership positions. You'll cast your bread upon the waters if you know you'll get returns. You have a great capacity for hard work and ability to run complicated operations.

Jupiter in Aquarius

You're the soul of good fellowship, surrounded by friends. You're lucky in group situations. You're great at innovative projects that have some social or humanitarian implications; in fact, you may have so many dreams and ideas that you may have trouble choosing one to implement. You're lucky in work that calls for inventiveness and gives you a great deal of freedom. The nine-to-five grind would drive you crazy.

Jupiter in Pisces

You're lucky when you're touching others' emotions, stirring their feelings. Or when you are helping the less fortunate. The theater, charity work, religious work, healing or helping professions all give you the chance to give emotionally. You may also have luck in work having to do with the sea, music, dance, footwear or any design work that encourages fantasy.

7

Uranus, Neptune and Pluto: The Power Planets

All the planets we've discussed so far have been known to astrologers for centuries; you can spot them easily on a clear night with the naked eye. We've seen how their forces can touch our personal lives on a daily basis. Now we come to the last three planets—Uranus, Neptune and Pluto—which astrologers call the "modern" planets, because they were not discovered until after the 17th century when it was possible to search the heavens with powerful telescopes.

As a group, these planets touch the "outer" boundaries of your life. They influence the revolutions, mass movements, dreams and sweeping concepts that characterize a whole generation. Each has unique physical characteristics that clue us to its character. The huge green Uranus seems to be orbiting on its side, with an eccentric tilted axis, surrounded by a herd of 15 moons, at last count by the Voyager 2 spacecraft. Astrologers designated it ruler of Aquarius, the sign that governs group activities and unpredictable events.

Neptune is also a giant swirling gaseous planet, so distant and greenish that only irregularities in the orbit of its neighbor, Uranus, hinted at its existence. This hide-and-seek planet rules Pisces, the sign of illusion.

Deepest in the solar system, remote Pluto is thought to be a tiny planet with an irregular orbit, yet unlike Neptune and Uranus, it is extremely dense and powerful. Its gravitational pull is strong enough to make its presence strongly felt by both its nearest neighbors. In fact, so little do we know about mysterious Pluto, that some scientists suspect that the actual planet may be quite large, and the only part visible to powerful telescopes is a small portion which reflects the distant light of the sun. Pluto's existence was ascertained only in 1930, when astrologers delegated it to Scorpio. But its gravitational pull was noted much earlier.

Astrologers refer to these planets as "the higher octave of the sun." As outlying planets, they transmit more intuitive, psychic and spiritual energies from outer space. But like the less-distant planets in your horoscope, they also touch you individually, both by their placement in the sky at the moment you were born and by their relationships with all the other planets at that time.

Uranus—The Shocker

Uranus rules intuition; it is your sixth sense, the part of you that is not ruled by external events. It cannot be "set up" or influenced by the past or by traditions or conventions. Thus it is often called the revolutionary or rebellious planet. It stays seven years in each of the 12 signs and signals where each generation rebels against the previous.

Uranus also rules electricity and when it hits a sensitive point in your chart, you are shocked out of a rut or at least given a surprise. Those influenced heavily by Uranus like to shock others. They aren't afraid to flout conventions, to parade their eccentricities. On the negative side, this is not a particularly sensitive, emotional planet. Uranians often use shock tactics without regard for stepping on toes.

The Uranus place in your horoscope is where you are liberated from the bonds of your personality or circumstances; where you are "free" or demand freedom; where you are original, march to your own drummer; where you have to do things *your* way, regardless of the prevailing rules and regulations.

The best thing about Uranus is the way it challenges you to discover yourself. A Uranus happening seems to say: Free yourself! You don't have to do things the way they were always done. Try something new, shake yourself up, open up to new things. It can be one of the most exciting times of your life, if you don't fight it by hanging on to the tried and true.

In 1988 Uranus is traveling back and forth between Sagittarius and Capricorn, which means these two signs will be especially affected. When it is in Sagittarius, it will also shake up Pisces, Gemini and Virgo. In Capricorn, it will touch Aries, Cancer and Libra.

Look up the sign of Uranus at the time of your birth and see where you follow your own tune—or that of your generation.

BIRTH DATE: March 31–November 4, 1927
       January 13, 1928–June 6, 1934
       October 10, 1934–March 28, 1935

Uranus in Aries
You're wide open about how you feel, and you won't be told what to do. Extremely individualistic, you tend to shoot off your mouth without thinking. This mixture of fire and electricity can be a real shocker.

BIRTH DATE: June 6, 1934–October 10, 1934
       March 28, 1935–August 7, 1941
       October 5, 1941–May 15, 1942

Uranus in Taurus
Here are the free-lance money earners, the original entrepreneurs. Money comes and goes in a flash. You may have sudden ups and downs in finances, but also lots of bright ideas that can lead to profit.

BIRTH DATE: August 7–October 5, 1941
              May 15, 1942–August 30, 1948
              November 12, 1948–June 10, 1949

Uranus in Gemini
The first television-influenced generation. This is the talk show in person: loads of advanced ideas, lots of skipping around suddenly and rushing about. But you may not be able to make those ideas actually happen unless you settle in with a solid structured organization.

BIRTH DATE: August 30–November 12, 1948
              June 10, 1949–August 24, 1955
              January 28–June 10, 1956

Uranus in Cancer
Many of you have had or will have an unconventional home atmosphere or unique, unstable living quarters. This influence could be manifested in frequent changes of residence or by working at home. You may feel very rebellious against your parents, feel rejected by them or break with them for some other reason. You tend to reject ties that bind and may postpone marriage and a family of your own.

BIRTH DATE: August 24, 1955–January 28, 1956
              June 10, 1956–November 1, 1961
              January 10–August 10, 1962

Uranus in Leo
You're on your own early with a great need to express

yourself creatively before an audience; the world must know about your great ideas. You may have some rather odd romances and unusual or gifted children.

BIRTH DATE: November 1, 1961–January 10, 1962
August 10, 1962–September 28, 1968
May 20, 1969–June 24, 1969

Uranus in Virgo

You have an unusual job or job schedule, or you may change jobs frequently. None of the conventional 9-to-5 routine for you. Several odd pets may share your life. And you may be vulnerable to psychosomatic illnesses.

BIRTH DATE: September 28, 1968–May 20, 1969
June 24, 1969–November 21, 1974
May 1–September 8, 1975

Uranus in Libra

You can't be tied down—better to have a bright relationship with lots of peers. Or else you may blame your partner for fencing you in. You can be attracted to unusual people or those of different races or cultures. Lots of divorces here.

BIRTH DATE: November 21, 1974–May 1, 1975
September 8, 1975–February 17, 1981
March 20–November 16, 1981

Uranus in Scorpio

Your birth time ushered in the sexual revolution. And you may have unconventional ideas about sex. You rebel against control of any kind. This placement can also bring unexpected windfalls, inheritances or traumatic events.

BIRTH DATE: February 17–March 20, 1981
November 16, 1981–February 15, 1988
May 27–Dec 2, 1988

Uranus in Sagittarius

You go for unusual forms of travel and make-your-own religions. You may mind travel via telepathy. Your generation may produce unusual forms of education.

BIRTH DATE: December 20, 1904–January 30, 1912
September 4–November 12, 1912
February 15–May 27, 1988
December 2, 1988–April 1, 1995
June 9, 1995–January 12, 1996

Uranus in Capricorn

You need plenty of psychic room. You may work alone or by computer. You're out to challenge and change the status quo. You're the one who really knows how to use computers in a practical way.

BIRTH DATE: January 30–September 4, 1912
November 12, 1912–April 1, 1919
August 16, 1919–January 22, 1920

Uranus in Aquarius

You think up odd ways to improve the world. You have a great tolerance for eccentricities. You're stimulated by unusual people around you. You have a need to experiment, find an unusual cause to embrace.

BIRTH DATE: April 1–August 16, 1919
January 22, 1920–March 31, 1927
November 4, 1927–January 13, 1928

Uranus in Pisces

This placement gives you great psychic radar. You're extremely intuitive and create in solitude listening to your inner voice. You use film in unique ways and can improvise with music. You rebel in emotional areas, with wildly original creative talent.

Neptune—The Dreamer

Neptune is the planet of dreams and fantasies. Officially discovered in 1846, it had been sighted several times in the previous fifty years, yet the astronomers simply did not believe their eyes. It became associated with illusion, delusion and deceit: those forces that dissolve our normal common sense and reason. It also rules inspiration, creativity and imagination, gifts that come with unselfishness and cannot be bought or learned.

A good Neptune placement will open doors between inspiration and reality. It will materialize inspiration in the form of art, theater, poetry or film that take us into a fantasy world. All kinds of creative, wonderful illusions come under Neptune. This planet also brings the beautiful selfless qualities of compassion and empathy. Working in tandem with the moon, it gives us a true sensitivity and understanding of others.

But the negative side of Neptune can be as treacherous as it is seductive. Here is where you escape reality into a world of artificially induced illusions, with drugs and alcohol. Here is the con artist, the liar and swindler, the delusions of grandeur, the crossing of the fine line between extreme creativity and paranoia. A difficult Neptune with problematical relationships to other planets is a subtly undermining force in a horoscope.

Neptune remains in a sign for about 13 years, coloring the fantasy life of an entire generation. Look up your Neptune in the following lists of placements for this century to check if these insights ring true for you and your peers.

BIRTH DATE: July 19–December 25, 1901
May 21, 1902–September 23, 1914
December 13, 1914–July 19, 1915
March 19–May 2, 1916

Neptune in Cancer

Those born early in this century idealized home and tradition, extending this to their nation. As Cancer rules emotions, it's no surprise that during this time emotions merited serious study. The Oedipal theories of Freud and the dream theories of Jung are particularly "Cancerian."

BIRTH DATE: September 23–December 14, 1914
July 19, 1915–March 19, 1916
May 2, 1916–September 21, 1928
February 19–July 24, 1929

Neptune in Leo

This was the "roaring twenties." A romantic, dramatic time with lots of illicit relationships, bootleg gin, the rise of Hollywood, grandiose dreams and big spenders.

BIRTH DATE: September 21, 1928–February 19, 1929
July 24, 1929–October 3, 1942
April 17–August 2, 1943

Neptune in Virgo

The great depression and the rise of the working class. This generation produced the health movement, the healers, the health food freaks, the Jane Fondas who brought glamour to exercise and being healthy.

BIRTH DATE: October 2, 1942–April 17, 1943
August 2, 1943–December 24, 1955
March 12–October 9, 1956
June 15–August 6, 1957

Neptune in Libra

This generation became the flower children, glamorizing "peace, love and joy." Odd partners and associates or a very unrealistic view of partnerships often characterize their life-styles. The United Nations was born during this time.

BIRTH DATE: August 6, 1957–January 4, 1970
May 3–November 6, 1970

Neptune in Scorpio
In the sixties this combination brought unusual sexual fantasies, interest in the occult, hallucinogenic drugs and the Vietnam War. This generation is now in its twenties and faced with another Neptunian drug temptation, cocaine. Some are reacting in an extreme way to the increase in sexually transmitted diseases by renouncing sex altogether.

BIRTH DATE: January 4–May 3, 1970
November 6, 1970–January 19, 1984
June 23–November 21, 1984

Neptune in Sagittarius
These dates brought outer space freaks. And a great religious revival, in all religions. Religion is now glamorized on television where evangelists vie with talk show hosts for large audiences. This generation will travel widely and be fascinated by mysticism, oriental religions and the spiritual life.

BIRTH DATE: January 19, 1984–June 23, 1984
November 21, 1984–January 29, 1998

Neptune in Capricorn
Having entered in 1984, Neptune will stay there until 1998, heralding a new conservatism and glamorizing work and success, the "yuppie" and the workaholic. This is also a time of scandals in the workplace. This generation may have unrealistic career objectives. Its members may do best in glamorous or helping profes-

sions—the more selfless work or a job where dreams can be realized in the marketplace.

Pluto—The Extremist

Nobody has seen much of Pluto, but we have all certainly felt the effects of this powerful little planet. Located for certain in 1930, the year Hitler rose to power and the time of the discovery of atomic energy, Pluto was given many of the attributes of the events at that time—an undercurrent of tremendous power that changes the shape of events, a latent violence, a drive for power. This planet has an extraordinary elliptical orbit that sometimes swings inside the orbit of Neptune. And it jogs in and out of signs, back and forth, spending from 12 to 31 years in each sign.

In astrology, Pluto is the planet of extremes and ruler of Scorpio. It may be invisible, but it is far from shy and retiring. Pluto is where you insist, where you won't compromise. In your chart, Pluto shows where you will go to extremes.

When Pluto hits a sensitive spot in your horoscope, there will be radical long-term changes. You'll have to get back to the basics, face the areas where you've been deceiving yourself, and change them for better or for worse. Pluto will transform anything it touches.

Since this far-out little planet takes about 234 years to circle the zodiac, and its weird elliptical orbit can keep it anywhere from 12 to 31 years in one sign, only 7 of the zodiac signs will be honored by its presence in this century. It traveled back and forth in Cancer and Gemini until 1937. Then Cancer and Leo until 1956. Leo, Virgo and Libra were home until 1983, when Pluto entered the sign it rules, Scorpio. After a brief visit back to Libra in 1984, it alternates between Scorpio and Sagittarius until the end of the century.

Who'll be feeling the power of Pluto in 1988? Pluto in Scorpio will particularly affect those Scorpios born in the first week of November of any year. And those born in the first weeks of May (Taurus), August (Leo) and February (Aquarius). Note changes in your life at this time! You can find your Pluto placement by checking your birthday with the travels of Pluto in this century, listed after each of the following descriptions.

Pluto in Cancer
This was a time of emotional power over the masses. Melodramas, sob story movies, the soap operas were hits then. Over-possessive mothers and nationalist leaders and dictators who extolled the glory of the motherland and the first women's rights activists were all part of this time. Deep sentimental feelings and strong patriotism characterized this generation.

BIRTH DATE: September 10–October 20, 1912
　　　　　　　July 9–December 28, 1913
　　　　　　　May 26, 1914–October 7, 1937
　　　　　　　February 7–June 14, 1939

Pluto in Leo
Here were the hippies, the dramatic "me" generation. These are the people who insist on getting their own way, doing their own thing. It is the generation who invented rock and roll.

BIRTH DATE: October 7–November 25, 1937
　　　　　　　August 3, 1938–February 7, 1939
　　　　　　　June 14, 1939–October 20, 1956
　　　　　　　January 15–August 19, 1957
　　　　　　　April 11–June 10, 1958

Pluto in Virgo
Here's the health movement, aerobics, fitness on a mass

scale. You want to be perfect and you want to work. This is the time of workaholics and computers who do all the detailed chores perfectly.

BIRTH DATE: October 20, 1956–January 15, 1957
                 August 19, 1957–April 11, 1958
                 June 10, 1958–October 5, 1971
                 April 17, 1971–July 30, 1972

Pluto in Libra

These people, now in their teens, will have some interesting ideas about partnerships and marriage. Idealistic romantic love will return. This group wants a beautiful, "true" relationship. The 70's and early 80's brought wide-reaching legislation: ERA, gay rights, abortion and equal opportunity laws. It also brought social forms of therapy: encounter groups, consciousness—raising groups, dialogue therapy.

BIRTH DATE: October 5, 1971–April 17, 1972
                 July 30, 1972–November 5, 1983
                 May 18–August 26, 1984

Pluto in Scorpio

In 1983 the planet returned to its home sign. This brought a reexamination of sexual attitudes, thanks to sexually transmitted diseases like AIDS and herpes and a prevalence of addictive drugs. A new wave of terrorism and nuclear leaks made news and will continue to do so, as if to say: it's time to clean up our act—and pay the price of our passions. Pluto in Scorpio may also bring the cure of the century's virulent diseases. There will also be a new understanding of death and the transcendence of death, with an emphasis on channeling through spiritual entities and trance mediums. Heavy metal music and "punks" are also signs of Pluto in Scorpio.

BIRTH DATE: November 5, 1983–May 18, 1984
              August 28, 1984–January 16, 1995
              April 21–November 10, 1995

Pluto in Sagittarius
This conjunction will finish the century, entering that
sign in 1995. This will bring a time of great mass
expansion. Space travel may now be a reality. Along
with this, a big emphasis on religion, spirituality and
philosophy, the higher meaning of life. On a mundane
level, gambling, travel and risk-taking bring the century to close with an optimistic view of the future.

8

Your Horoscope:
A Personal Star Map

What Is a Horoscope?

When you hear terms like "charts," "rising signs," "houses" and "aspects" tossed around, you may realize that astrology has a complex vocabulary of its own, one that is often baffling and confusing to the layman. Yet the basic concept is very simple. A horoscope is a map of a moment in time. Someone could be born at this moment. Or there could be an important event taking place. In fact, anything can have a horoscope: countries, business deals, stocks, pets, trips, a question to be answered, a love affair, a marriage.

Astrology is based on the assumption that each moment in time is unique and imprints itself on the person or event taking place. The horoscope, its basic tool, charts where the sun, moon and planets were located at the exact moment that the person, place or thing was "born." That is why it is critically important to know the exact time of the horoscope. Two maps done moments apart can have significant differences to the trained eye.

When you first see a horoscope, you may wonder what this strange diagram is all about. It is a circle divided into twelve segments like a pizza, a cake or a wagon wheel. In each of the slices are strange looking symbols called "glyphs" which represent the astrological signs and the planets. Each planet and sign has its own special identifying glyph, which astrologers use as a form of shorthand.

The center of the wheel represents the earth and is bisected horizontally by the local horizon line. Above the horizon is the "daylight" half of the horoscope— every planet on the top half of the horoscope appeared in the sky overhead when the horoscope was cast. The bottom or "nighttime" half of the horoscope represents the sky visible to the other half of the earth. Therefore, the sun would be in the "nighttime" or bottom half if you were born in the evening.

A House Is a Slice of Life

The sky is divided up into twelve separate "slices" of life called "houses." Each slice has the character of an astrological sign—the first slice deals with Aries-like matters, the second Taurus, the third Gemini, etc. The planets fall into these houses depending on their location in the sky at that moment. For instance, if the chart is for noontime, the sun would be directly at the top of the wheel, in the ninth or tenth house. At midnight, the sun would be at the bottom of the wheel in the third or fourth house.

How the Planets Move through the Horoscope

As the zodiac moves through the sky during the day, the signs pass over each house. In May Taurus would pass over the first house around dawn, over the tenth house at the top of the chart around noon, over the sixth house on the horizon at sunset. Yet the second house, which embodies the characteristics of Taurus, would still remain in its original place below the horizon.

Planets Live in Signs, but Travel through Houses

The planets have both a sign and a house. It's very easy to confuse the two terms. The *sign* of the planet is its location in the zodiac, in space. The *house* of the planet in its location in the sky relative to the earth's orbit and your local horizon. For example a planet such as Venus might be passing through the sign of Taurus. But the sign of Taurus would rotate through all twelve houses during the day. So at dawn, Venus in Taurus would be on the horizon in the first house; at 3 p.m., in the eighth house; by 8 p.m., it would have traveled below the horizon into the sixth house. (The zodiac moves clockwise, the houses counter-clockwise in order with the bottom or evening houses numbered first.) Remember that the planets all stay on the same zodiac pathway, called the "ecliptic"; they don't wander off into other constellations like the Big Dipper or Orion.

The zodiac rotates from left to right on the chart. The left side of the horizontal line that bisects the chart is called the "ascendant" or the "rising sign." That is the zodiac sign on the horizon at the moment the chart was cast. Imagine the horoscope as a clock with the hands set at 9:40. This slice would be the first house and the rising sign would be the hour hand set at 9. The rising sign is the leader of the horoscope; it sets up the signs on the borderline or "cusps" of the other eleven houses. Since the planets change signs approximately every two hours, the signs on the cusps change also, altering the character of each house.

The opposite or sunset point of the chart is called the "descendant." "Midheaven" is the noontime or highest point of the chart, and the "nadir" is the midnight or lowest point of the chart. These are the most critical points of the horoscope.

What the Houses Mean

Though each house has the characteristics of a zodiac

105

sign, it is also colored by the sign rotating over the house at the moment the chart is cast. For instance, the second house rules Taurus-influenced things—finances and material resources, safety and security. If Leo were passing over this house at the time of day the chart was cast, this would alter the house, giving it Leo's generosity and "big spender" traits—and a tendency to take a big gamble.

The house is also influenced by the planets located in its portion of the sky. A group of planets in the same house gives that area of life great importance.

The first three houses have to do with self-expression, first impressions, personal resources and mental structure. The next three involve relationships with the family: the home or foundation, the children and creativity, the day-to-day maintenance and support. The seventh through tenth houses deal with social consequences, marriage or partnerships, the productivity or fertility of relationships, and the aspirations for the future. The last three houses deal with the most impersonal matters: career and social position; group relationships; detachment, isolation and "karma."

Here is a rundown of the meaning of each house.

FIRST HOUSE: Your outward expression, physical body, the way you come across to the world. The natural place for Aries and the planet Mars.

SECOND HOUSE: Your material and business dealings. Business, money, financial security, things you buy. The rewards of your personal efforts. The best place for Taurus and the planet Venus.

THIRD HOUSE: Your mental ability—how your mind works in the immediate environment. Your neighbors and close friends, daily communications, short trips, short written works. Gemini and Mercury rule this house.

FOURTH HOUSE: The home base of life, your family foundation, the final resting place. It's the natural place for Cancer and the moon.

FIFTH HOUSE: Your creative resources, romantic love nature, friends, playmates. How you express yourself creatively, after your personality is established. The sign of Leo and the sun are at home here.

SIXTH HOUSE: General health, chores and detail work, pets, service jobs. The necessary tasks to make things work. The natural home of Virgo and Mercury.

SEVENTH HOUSE: Partnerships, open relationships with others, marriage, open enemies, business partnerships. The natural home of Libra and Venus.

EIGHTH HOUSE: How you use other people's resources: money you do not earn directly, such as benefits brought by marriage or partnerships, legacies. The house of Scorpio and Pluto-influenced things: great changes, sex, life-and-death matters, psychology, and the occult.

NINTH HOUSE: Where you expand your mind via foreign travel, higher education, publishing, religion, aspirations; how you spread your work to the world. The "big picture." The natural place for Sagittarius and Jupiter.

TENTH HOUSE: Reputation, career, public image. Your most dominant parent, your status symbols, your attitude toward authority. The home of Capricorn and Saturn.

ELEVENTH HOUSE: Your Aquarius-type social connections, your peer group. Where you apply yourself to humanity at large; what you do to save the world, clubs, other people's children. The Uranus influence on far-out hopes and dreams.

TWELFTH HOUSE: Where you are alone in the world. Your secret inner self, the hidden things in your life, your escapist tendencies, your karma, how you overcome restrictions. Also secluded places of residence, monasteries, hospitals and prisons. The way you give with no idea of return, how you do emotional service. Your secret enemies. The influence of Pisces and the planet Neptune.

What an Astrologer Looks For

An astrologer will look first at the general overall distribution of the planets in the sky. The majority of planets above the horizon tend to reveal that the person will be more in the public life. Planets below the horizon mean a more private person, who works behind the scenes. A majority of planets to the right of center indicate a person who depends on others to survive, who is something of a fatalist; to the left of center, a more self-directed take-charge type.

After locating the planets and the signs on the house cusps, an astrologer will look for relationships between the planets, called "aspects." There are some aspects which make life easy for the subject. Energies flow smoothly between the planetary forces; they seem to be helping each other out.

Other aspects create tension. It's as if the planets are challenging each other or working at cross-purposes. The subject will have to work to resolve conflicts here.

An aspect is actually a term for a distance between two forces within the 360-degree circle. The sextile (60 degrees apart) and the trine (120 degrees) are considered harmonious. The square (90 degrees) is a hard angle (you're squaring off) and the opposition (180 degrees) is pulling in the opposite direction.

Usually you'll find at least two or more celestial bodies in the horoscope placed closely together; this is called a conjunction. Here, different forces are traveling together in the same house, for better or for worse. Some like the sun and Venus, get along well together, others like Uranus and Mars have an uneasy alliance at best. Sometimes there are several crowding one house, which can make the activities in that house and the relationships to it dominate the horoscope.

ASPECTS OF THE SUN AFFECT: self-expression, your physical body, your courage and energy.

ASPECTS OF THE MOON AFFECT: intense feelings, emotional growth, the unconscious, your maternal instinct, your female emotional ideal.

ASPECTS OF MERCURY AFFECT: what interests you, how your mind works.

ASPECTS OF VENUS AFFECT: how you relate to others, your sense of beauty.

ASPECTS OF MARS AFFECT: your temper, aggressive instincts, possible violence, driving energy.

ASPECTS OF JUPITER AFFECT: good fortune, opportunities, expansion.

ASPECTS OF SATURN AFFECT: restrictions, selfishness, rigidity, discipline.

ASPECTS OF NEPTUNE AFFECT: how you face reality, your dreams, self-delusions, forms of escape.

ASPECTS OF URANUS AFFECT: sudden changes, originality, eccentricity, flouting of convention.

ASPECTS OF PLUTO AFFECT: mass power, transforming incidents, sexual charisma, willpower.

Much of the positive or negative effects of the aspects depends on the houses and the signs involved and how much the planets are "at home" in their environment. An astrologer is constantly weighing these variables. Nobody has—or wants—a chart full of the easy aspects, where there are no challenges or learning experiences. Squares and oppositions not only mean tension, they indicate excitement, sex appeal, action. A lawyer, a police officer, a politician, a football player needs some fighting spirit! Whether you're a prize fighter or a street gangster, a drifter or a diplomat depends on your circumstances and how you use these energies in your career and personal relationships.

There are many different types of horoscopes. A chart based on your birthday, which is your basic character, always remains the same. In addition, astrologers often do a chart based on the changes since the time you were born, called a "progressed" chart, to bring you up to date.

If you are contemplating a close partnership or a

love relationship, you can have a "synastry" chart done which compares both charts and can zero in on potential problem areas. You'll want to watch the Mars, Venus and moon aspects in an emotional relationship to see if your tastes are similar and you can express your feelings and excite each other. In business you'll consider Mercury, Mars, Saturn and Jupiter relationships for attitudes toward spending, temperament, communication and sense of responsibility.

What's Happening Now—The Transits

Throughout your life, the planets will be constantly moving around the zodiac, affecting each placement in your horoscope. Every time a planet passes your sun, moon and so forth, you will feel it in some way. These sensitive times are called "transits." The fast-moving moon hits every one of your planets once a month, constantly squaring, opposing or trining each force in your life—which accounts, astrologically, for your many moods. You can follow your moon-mood changes in the daily forecasts in the back of this book. A Venus transit is something to look forward to as you become more attractive to others. Uranus brings sudden surprises; Mars a burst of energy or anger; Saturn a test or restriction; Mercury brings news; Pluto a major change.

Your horoscope is an invaluable tool for navigating through life. It can give you tips, guidance, point out difficulties, help you find a mate, advise you when to stay home or go out and socialize. But it cannot control you. Even the most detailed weather map won't help you if you don't take advantage of the good winds or pull into port in a storm. So, if you know you're in for a time of testing, gear up to learn. If you're in for a shake-up, open your mind to new possibilities, and if communications are stalled, use the time to reevaluate your plans.

9

How Others See You:
Your Rising Sign

The first impression you make on others has much to do with your rising sign—the sign on the eastern horizon at the time you were born. In a sense, it is like a mask you wear which can be very different from your sun sign's "face," particularly if the sign is of a different element. A slow-moving earth sign like Taurus could appear far more dynamic with a fire sign like Aries or Sagittarius rising. A Gemini with Scorpio rising is likely to come across with the intense conviction and stinging sarcasm of the Scorpio rather than the light wit of a Gemini.

Like many people, you may have been born in the early morning when your sun sign was rising. This gives you the outward expression and charisma of your sun—there will be no mistaking you for another sign. You'll assert yourself, dress, walk and use the gestures of your sun.

You must know the time of your birth to determine the exact rising sign, because the *degree* of the rising sign or "ascendent," as it is also called, changes every four minutes and the rising sign *itself* changes every two hours. If you are not sure—or you know only the approximate hour, given a two-hour leeway, you can make a good guess with the help of the chart on pages 116–117.

If the rising signs listed here do not seem to agree with your appearance and mannerisms, check the descriptions of the rising signs preceding and following. It is very possible that your timing may be an hour or so off, and your true colors will show up in another place.

Scorpio with Aries Rising
What energy! You make your presence immediately felt. Yet you are not as open and aboveboard as you may seem, in spite of your assertive, confrontational style. There's a lot you're *not* saying.

Scorpio with Taurus Rising
You can seem like an immovable object. Stubborn is your middle name. Yet your reverse side is soft, sensual and mellow. You love to overindulge in everything that feels, tastes, looks, sounds and smells good.

Scorpio with Gemini Rising
You hide your deep feeling nature behind a great gift of gab. Everything about you is animated and expressive. People might get confused when they learn how very much you care.

Scorpio with Cancer Rising
Moody and brooding, especially at the full moon, you seem to withdraw into yourself. You are really not that shy—just finding a safe vantage point from which to check out the situation. You rarely say what you feel, maybe because you feel a lot.

Scorpio with Leo Rising
With your commanding presence, it's hard not to take over immediately. The world's a stage and you're the

star. A toss of the regal mane, a radiant smile and a cleft chin come with the territory.

Scorpio with Virgo Rising
You are the master of stinging criticism and scrupulous faultfinding. Your sharp eyes don't miss a flaw. You care deeply about matters of health, cleanliness, order and organization. And you like being of service. Show others how much you care by being more tolerant of their shortcomings.

Scorpio with Libra Rising
Your calm and charming demeanor belie your intense inner life. Your winning hand probably includes good looks, a smooth way with words, excellent taste and style. No wonder you attract the opposite sex in droves.

Scorpio with Scorpio Rising
You're a walking mystery that gives out no clues. Who knows what you're all about, you fascinating devil! Many of the opposite sex would love to unravel you. You magnetize them at a glance. It's all or nothing!

Scorpio with Sagittarius Rising
You're a happy-go-lucky playboy on the surface. But underneath, you're far more heavy going. Your blunt remarks hit the bulls eye, and often cut deep. But your strong legs and stamina make you a terrific athlete.

Scorpio with Capricorn Rising
Male or female, you look like a boss. Natural dignity, strong bone structure and a melancholy air give you aristocratic appeal. Your eye for quality makes you look rich, no mtter what your financial state.

Scorpio with Aquarius Rising
You can seem distant and remote, except in groups, when you magically come alive. You speak your mind

and secretly enjoy shocking people. People never know what you're going to do next. You appear to avoid one-on-one relationships, arranging to be "alone in the crowd."

Scorpio with Pisces Rising
You'll play whatever role is required to stay on top of the situation. The opposite sex usually responds with enthusiasm. But some folks may wonder where the real you is hiding. Reveal yourself once in a while, for the sake of sincerity and trust.

How to Find Your Rising Sign

To find your accurate rising sign, you should know the exact time of your birth. But even though this is not always possible, you can make a good guess with the help of the following chart.

Look down the list on the left side of the chart for the birthday nearest yours. The year is not important. Then look across the top of the chart for the time nearest your birth time. The A.M. times are listed on the left page, the P.M. times on the right. If daylight savings time was in effect, you should subtract one hour from the time on the chart. Follow this column down until you reach the nearest birth date; the sign abbreviated in that place should be your rising sign.

Since the signs change approximately every two hours, you should check the signs before and after your estimated rising sign. For instance, if you were born on March 11 at about 6:15 a.m., your rising sign would most likely be Pisces. But read the description for Aries as well and note if this seems more like you.

The geographical latitude also affects your rising sign. These tables were calculated for the middle latitudes of the United States. If you were born far to the south, look at the sign that follows your rising sign as well. If you were born far to the north or in Canada, check out the previous sign.

Rising Signs—A.M. Births

	1 AM	2 AM	3 AM	4 AM	5 AM	6 AM	7 AM	8 AM	9 AM	10 AM	11 AM	12 NOON
Jan 1	Lib	Sc	Sc	Sc	Sag	Sag	Cap	Cap	Aq	Aq	Pis	Ar
Jan 9	Lib	Sc	Sc	Sag	Sag	Sag	Cap	Cap	Aq	Pis	Ar	Tau
Jan 17	Sc	Sc	Sc	Sag	Sag	Cap	Cap	Aq	Aq	Pis	Ar	Tau
Jan 25	Sc	Sc	Sag	Sag	Sag	Cap	Cap	Aq	Pis	Ar	Tau	Tau
Feb 2	Sc	Sc	Sag	Sag	Cap	Cap	Aq	Pis	Pis	Ar	Tau	Gem
Feb 10	Sc	Sag	Sag	Sag	Cap	Cap	Aq	Pis	Ar	Tau	Tau	Gem
Feb 18	Sc	Sag	Sag	Cap	Cap	Aq	Pis	Pis	Ar	Tau	Gem	Gem
Feb 26	Sag	Sag	Sag	Cap	Aq	Aq	Pis	Ar	Tau	Tau	Gem	Gem
Mar 6	Sag	Sag	Cap	Cap	Aq	Pis	Pis	Ar	Tau	Gem	Gem	Can
Mar 14	Sag	Cap	Cap	Aq	Aq	Pis	Ar	Tau	Tau	Gem	Gem	Can
Mar 22	Sag	Cap	Cap	Aq	Pis	Ar	Ar	Tau	Gem	Gem	Can	Can
Mar 30	Cap	Cap	Aq	Pis	Pis	Ar	Tau	Tau	Gem	Can	Can	Can
Apr 7	Cap	Cap	Aq	Pis	Ar	Ar	Tau	Gem	Gem	Can	Can	Leo
Apr 14	Cap	Aq	Aq	Pis	Ar	Tau	Tau	Gem	Gem	Can	Can	Leo
Apr 22	Cap	Aq	Pis	Ar	Ar	Tau	Gem	Gem	Can	Can	Leo	Leo
Apr 30	Aq	Aq	Pis	Ar	Tau	Tau	Gem	Can	Can	Can	Leo	Leo
May 8	Aq	Pis	Ar	Ar	Tau	Gem	Gem	Can	Can	Leo	Leo	Leo
May 16	Aq	Pis	Ar	Tau	Gem	Gem	Can	Can	Can	Leo	Leo	Vir
May 24	Pis	Ar	Ar	Tau	Gem	Gem	Can	Can	Leo	Leo	Leo	Vir
June 1	Pis	Ar	Tau	Gem	Gem	Can	Can	Can	Leo	Leo	Vir	Vir
June 9	Ar	Ar	Tau	Gem	Gem	Can	Can	Leo	Leo	Leo	Vir	Vir
June 17	Ar	Tau	Gem	Gem	Can	Can	Can	Leo	Leo	Vir	Vir	Vir
June 25	Tau	Tau	Gem	Gem	Can	Can	Leo	Leo	Leo	Vir	Vir	Lib
July 3	Tau	Gem	Gem	Can	Can	Can	Leo	Leo	Vir	Vir	Vir	Lib
July 11	Tau	Gem	Gem	Can	Can	Leo	Leo	Leo	Vir	Vir	Lib	Lib
July 18	Gem	Gem	Can	Can	Can	Leo	Leo	Vir	Vir	Vir	Lib	Lib
July 26	Gem	Gem	Can	Can	Leo	Leo	Vir	Vir	Vir	Lib	Lib	Lib
Aug 3	Gem	Can	Can	Can	Leo	Leo	Vir	Vir	Vir	Lib	Lib	Sc
Aug 11	Gem	Can	Can	Leo	Leo	Leo	Vir	Vir	Lib	Lib	Lib	Sc
Aug 18	Can	Can	Can	Leo	Leo	Vir	Vir	Vir	Lib	Lib	Sc	Sc
Aug 27	Can	Can	Leo	Leo	Leo	Vir	Vir	Lib	Lib	Lib	Sc	Sc
Sept 4	Can	Can	Leo	Leo	Leo	Vir	Vir	Vir	Lib	Lib	Sc	Sc
Sept 12	Can	Leo	Leo	Leo	Vir	Vir	Lib	Lib	Lib	Sc	Sc	Sag
Sept 30	Leo	Leo	Leo	Vir	Vir	Vir	Lib	Lib	Sc	Sc	Sc	Sag
Sept 28	Leo	Leo	Leo	Vir	Vir	Lib	Lib	Lib	Sc	Sc	Sag	Sag
Oct 6	Leo	Leo	Vir	Vir	Vir	Lib	Lib	Sc	Sc	Sc	Sag	Sag
Oct 14	Leo	Vir	Vir	Vir	Lib	Lib	Lib	Sc	Sc	Sag	Sag	Cap
Oct 22	Leo	Vir	Vir	Lib	Lib	Lib	Sc	Sc	Sc	Sag	Sag	Cap
Oct 30	Vir	Vir	Vir	Lib	Lib	Sc	Sc	Sc	Sag	Sag	Cap	Cap
Nov 7	Vir	Vir	Lib	Lib	Lib	Sc	Sc	Sc	Sag	Sag	Cap	Cap
Nov 15	Vir	Vir	Lib	Lib	Sc	Sc	Sc	Sag	Sag	Cap	Cap	Aq
Nov 23	Vir	Lib	Lib	Lib	Sc	Sc	Sag	Sag	Sag	Cap	Cap	Aq
Dec 1	Vir	Lib	Lib	Sc	Sc	Sc	Sag	Sag	Cap	Cap	Aq	Aq
Dec 9	Lib	Lib	Lib	Sc	Sc	Sag	Sag	Sag	Cap	Cap	Aq	Pis
Dec 18	Lib	Lib	Sc	Sc	Sc	Sag	Sag	Cap	Cap	Aq	Aq	Pis
Dec 28	Lib	Lib	Sc	Sc	Sag	Sag	Sag	Cap	Aq	Aq	Pis	Ar

Rising Signs—P.M. Births

	1 PM	2 PM	3 PM	4 PM	5 PM	6 PM	7 PM	8 PM	9 PM	10 PM	11 PM	12 MIDNIGHT
Jan 1	Tau	Gem	Gem	Can	Can	Can	Leo	Leo	Vir	Vir	Vir	Lib
Jan 9	Tau	Gem	Gem	Can	Can	Leo	Leo	Leo	Vir	Vir	Vir	Lib
Jan 17	Gem	Gem	Can	Can	Can	Leo	Leo	Vir	Vir	Vir	Lib	Lib
Jan 25	Gem	Gem	Can	Can	Leo	Leo	Leo	Vir	Vir	Lib	Lib	Lib
Feb 2	Gem	Can	Can	Can	Leo	Leo	Vir	Vir	Vir	Lib	Lib	Sc
Feb 10	Gem	Can	Can	Leo	Leo	Leo	Vir	Vir	Lib	Lib	Lib	Sc
Feb 18	Can	Can	Can	Leo	Leo	Vir	Vir	Vir	Lib	Lib	Sc	Sc
Feb 26	Can	Can	Leo	Leo	Leo	Vir	Vir	Lib	Lib	Lib	Sc	Sc
Mar 6	Can	Leo	Leo	Leo	Vir	Vir	Vir	Lib	Lib	Sc	Sc	Sc
Mar 14	Can	Leo	Leo	Vir	Vir	Vir	Lib	Lib	Lib	Sc	Sc	Sag
Mar 22	Leo	Leo	Leo	Vir	Vir	Lib	Lib	Lib	Sc	Sc	Sc	Sag
Mar 30	Leo	Leo	Vir	Vir	Vir	Lib	Lib	Sc	Sc	Sc	Sag	Sag
Apr 7	Leo	Leo	Vir	Vir	Lib	Lib	Lib	Sc	Sc	Sc	Sag	Sag
Apr 14	Leo	Vir	Vir	Vir	Lib	Lib	Sc	Sc	Sc	Sag	Sag	Cap
Apr 22	Leo	Vir	Vir	Lib	Lib	Lib	Sc	Sc	Sc	Sag	Sag	Cap
Apr 30	Vir	Vir	Vir	Lib	Lib	Sc	Sc	Sc	Sag	Sag	Cap	Cap
May 8	Vir	Vir	Lib	Lib	Lib	Sc	Sc	Sag	Sag	Sag	Cap	Cap
May 16	Vir	Vir	Lib	Lib	Sc	Sc	Sc	Sag	Sag	Cap	Cap	Aq
May 24	Vir	Lib	Lib	Lib	Sc	Sc	Sag	Sag	Sag	Cap	Cap	Aq
June 1	Vir	Lib	Lib	Sc	Sc	Sc	Sag	Sag	Cap	Cap	Aq	Aq
June 9	Lib	Lib	Lib	Sc	Sc	Sag	Sag	Sag	Cap	Cap	Aq	Pis
June 17	Lib	Lib	Sc	Sc	Sc	Sag	Sag	Cap	Cap	Aq	Aq	Pis
June 25	Lib	Lib	Sc	Sc	Sag	Sag	Sag	Cap	Cap	Aq	Pis	Ar
July 3	Lib	Sc	Sc	Sc	Sag	Sag	Cap	Cap	Aq	Aq	Pis	Ar
July 11	Lib	Sc	Sc	Sag	Sag	Sag	Cap	Cap	Aq	Pis	Ar	Tau
July 18	Sc	Sc	Sc	Sag	Sag	Cap	Cap	Aq	Aq	Pis	Ar	Tau
July 26	Sc	Sc	Sag	Sag	Sag	Cap	Cap	Aq	Pis	Ar	Tau	Tau
Aug 3	Sc	Sc	Sag	Sag	Cap	Cap	Aq	Aq	Pis	Ar	Tau	Gem
Aug 11	Sc	Sag	Sag	Sag	Cap	Cap	Aq	Pis	Ar	Tau	Tau	Gem
Aug 18	Sc	Sag	Sag	Cap	Cap	Aq	Pis	Pis	Ar	Tau	Gem	Gem
Aug 27	Sag	Sag	Sag	Cap	Cap	Aq	Pis	Ar	Tau	Tau	Gem	Gem
Sept 4	Sag	Sag	Cap	Cap	Aq	Pis	Pis	Ar	Tau	Gem	Gem	Can
Sept 12	Sag	Sag	Cap	Aq	Aq	Pis	Ar	Tau	Tau	Gem	Gem	Can
Sept 20	Sag	Cap	Cap	Aq	Pis	Pis	Ar	Tau	Gem	Gem	Can	Can
Sept 28	Cap	Cap	Aq	Aq	Pis	Ar	Tau	Tau	Gem	Gem	Can	Can
Oct 6	Cap	Cap	Aq	Pis	Ar	Ar	Tau	Gem	Gem	Can	Can	Leo
Oct 14	Cap	Aq	Aq	Pis	Ar	Tau	Tau	Gem	Gem	Can	Can	Leo
Oct 22	Cap	Aq	Pis	Ar	Ar	Tau	Gem	Gem	Can	Can	Leo	Leo
Oct 30	Aq	Aq	Pis	Ar	Tau	Tau	Gem	Can	Can	Can	Leo	Leo
Nov 7	Aq	Aq	Pis	Ar	Tau	Tau	Gem	Can	Can	Can	Leo	Leo
Nov 15	Aq	Pis	Ar	Tau	Gem	Gem	Can	Can	Can	Leo	Leo	Vir
Nov 23	Pis	Ar	Ar	Tau	Gem	Gem	Can	Can	Leo	Leo	Leo	Vir
Dec 1	Pis	Ar	Tau	Gem	Gem	Can	Can	Can	Leo	Leo	Vir	Vir
Dec 9	Ar	Tau	Tau	Gem	Gem	Can	Can	Leo	Leo	Leo	Vir	Vir
Dec 18	Ar	Tau	Gem	Gem	Can	Can	Can	Leo	Leo	Vir	Vir	Vir
Dec 28	Tau	Tau	Gem	Gem	Can	Can	Leo	Leo	Vir	Vir	Vir	Lib

10

How Astrology Can Help Your Relationships

Surely you've met the "odd couple" who defy conventional romantic stereotypes and wondered what brought them together. Why did the sexy hunk marry a prim librarian, what does the professor see in that bubbly blonde, how could the glamorous film star marry her accountant? Yet so many of these apparently mismatched pairs are obviously happy together. Then there are the magic couples like Elizabeth Taylor and Richard Burton that seemed to be meant for each other—how shocked we are when we read about their split-ups!

Those in love—or those who *wish* they were—often turn to astrology in their search for that elusive formula that will draw the right person and sustain the initial attraction. Their questions are endless: What sign is the best for me, will it last, can a Scorpio possibly make it with a Gemini?

Unfortunately, there are no pat answers. Even the most perfect star-cast relationship will have problem areas; on the other hand, even the most unlikely astrological combinations have a chance of success. Take the case of this "impossible" air and water sign combination: an Aquarian man, who lives in the public eye, married to a home-loving Cancer woman. Yet the loving marriage of Aquarian President Ronald Reagan and his Cancer wife, Nancy, sets a stellar standard of matrimonial success.

Astrology can help you know in advance prepare for the problems you're likely to encounter and to analyze your own wants and needs before you make a commitment.

Some Element-ary Facts:

When people say they have wonderful chemistry together—their romance has earthy sensuality, fiery passion, a meeting of minds or waves of emotion—they may well be making an astrological analogy. The quickest way to get a reading on a relationship is to compare the basic elements in your astrological signs. Though this will not illuminate the finer points, it will give you a good overall view of how you relate and where you may have to compromise to smooth out rough spots.

Imagine yourself and the person who attracts you as embodying the elements of your sun signs:

EARTH: Taurus, Virgo, Capricorn
AIR: Gemini, Libra, Aquarius
FIRE: Aries, Leo, Sagittarius
WATER: Cancer, Scorpio, Pisces

The interactions of these basic elements have many parallels to the interactions of each of the signs. In your romantic chemistry laboratory, you must find the right balance of these elements for the relationship to flourish.

Fiery Combinations
Can fire burn without fuel to nourish it? Fire and earth signs can build a bonfire together. Fire provides the

energy and enthusiasm, earth the organization and follow-through. But fire likes to spread and burn brightly; earth likes to put down roots. Earth signs also like to accumulate possessions, while fire likes to wander unfettered. You'll both have to adjust. Fire has to learn to provide security, earth to be flexible.

Fire and air will burn brightly, expending a great deal of energy. But too much air extinguishes fire, and too much fire suffocates air. You both need plenty of space to express yourselves. There could be lots of talk and no action with this combination.

Fire and water create emotional energy. This can be a very creative dramatic combination, with each inspiring the other. Yet fire can evaporate water with insensitivity and egotism, while water will extinguish fire's spirit with emotional manipulation. To make this work, fire must develop tact and sympathy. Water must not take everything to heart or drown fire's enthusiasm.

Fire with fire is either an explosion of energy or a burnout. This is a combination that needs to develop discipline and control. Since both like to get their own way and neither is quick to make adjustments there could be a serious clash of egos.

Earthy Passions
Sensual earth signs are often fascinated by the drama and enthusiasm of fire. And fire's get-up-and-go attitude gets these slow starters moving. But fire's lack of clear direction and impatience when the going gets rough could be a big turnoff. So could the tendency to take big risks without considering the consequences. It's usually up to earth to provide the steady support system and the steady income.

Earth and air often seem at cross-purposes. Air may find stolid practical earth signs boring, earth may find air a bit flaky. But earth can give substance to air signs, making their ideas actually happen. With a lot of give and take, you can accomplish much together.

Earth and water seem like a naturally good combination. But too much water makes mud. Earth signs get tired of caring for water signs' needs, while water feels smothered by earth's realistic attitude. You relate well and can patch up many differences on the sensual level, however.

Two earth signs understand each other beautifully, especially on a physical level. The problem here is complacency. Something has to move the mountain when you two stubborn signs dig in your heels.

Air Power

Air and fire signs can spark each other instantly. At first, you seem to bring out each other's best qualities. Your mental, flirtatious nature is just the challenge that fire signs need. You know how to play hard to get, which has them running in hot pursuit. Later on, it can be all talk and no action—or a lot of aimless running around. To make this work, you need maturity and clear-cut goals.

Air and earth signs may never see eye to eye. Earth wants to see concrete results, air likes to talk ideas and may never get down to business. Air gets bored easily and may find the slow going of earth giving a bad case of yawns. Earth's possessiveness is unbearable when air needs space to expand and explore. There's lots of adjusting for both of you.

Water and air signs can work beautifully on a mental level. Water's creativity and air's ideas and objectivity blend beautifully. It's when the water signs get soggy and emotional that air would rather breeze off. But if air can learn to open up and express its feelings and water can learn to give air enough freedom, the two can work things out.

Air and air exchange mental stimulation and understanding. But here's the problem of "all talk and no action." And both need to cultivate give and take on the emotional level or they'll wind up just not caring enough to commit themselves.

Water Lovers

Water signs take to earth signs naturally. At first earth seems to supply just what water needs—a strong foundation of support and stability to anchor your dreams. Plus lots of practical know-how. Not to mention delightful sensuality. There's a strong physical attraction. The trouble comes when earth signs get possessive and demanding, with no sympathy for water's procrastination and seeming lack of organization. The earth signs don't seem to understand why water signs need to dream so much. And water may find earth inflexible, unimaginative and preoccupied with mundane things— like possessions, keeping up with the neighbors and paying the rent.

Water and air will work if your partner's airy nature inspires you and provides objectivity. And air signs' sense of humor can banish the blues fast and get you out of your solitary mood and out among people again. They're great pals, but lovers? Heavy emotions blow them away fast, and they won't succumb to emotional manipulation and guilt trips either. They just take everything too lightly for you. If you're looking for depth and intensity, move on!

Water and fire can be terrific, if the fire gets water moving, making it do something about those dreams. The fire signs' natural confidence and courage bouys water up. And fire's salesmanship can push water to great heights. Water signs know how to flatter fire signs and appeal to their ego. The going is great until fire steps on water's toes. Not known for sensitivity, fire signs often bully to get their way, and run ruthlessly roughshod over water's feelings. And when water signs sit around moping—forget it! Fire is off and running—water may have trouble holding its own.

Water and water are soul mates. You can experience the deepest, most intense feelings with someone of our own element. That person can give you the tenderness you need and know how to soothe you when you've been battered by the outside world. The problems come when two water signs get into black moods. It's difficult to gain perspective and lift each other out of a depression. Both could tend to drown their sorrows in tears or alcohol—or wound each other deeply with cutting remarks (knowing just how to find where it really hurts.)

The Aspects of Love

Another way of dealing with relationships is to look for the right angles. In astrology that means the distance between the other person's sign and yours.

The easy angles: 60 degrees (sextile) or 120 degrees (trine) apart.

The trine and sextile aspects (located two and four signs away from yours) are the easiest for communications flow. You seem to share effortlessly, have fewer disagreements.

The challenges: 90 degrees (square) or 180 degrees (opposition) apart.

There is lots of stimulation in the square or opposition aspect. (These are located three and six signs away from yours.) You can turn each other on, in a sexy way, with never a dull moment—or work at cross purposes. It won't be easy to understand where the other person is coming from, but it could be interesting to find out. You'll grow and explore new territory here.

The next-door neighbors: These are the signs on either side of yours. There's a buddy relationship here; you both have something to give each other, even though you are not alike. It's not the sexy chemistry of the square or opposition, but it can be a very comfortable partnership.

Some Other Planetary Clues and Cues

Defining Your Needs with the Moon

The position of the moon at the time of your birth greatly influences your emotional reactions. And if your moon is in the same sign as your lover's sun or moon, you will have a deep emotional bond. The moon also affects the subconscious needs in our life, and since our strongest ties are subconscious, stemming back to our tie with our mother (also symbolized by the moon), a partner with a compatible moon sign can be a part of a very strong and lasting tie indeed. This bond will operate on an instinctive level; you'll feel drawn to moon-compatible people without quite understanding why.

Your moon in the same sign as your lover's moon is the best aspect for a long-lasting relationship. Moons in different signs, but in the *same element* are also harmonious. Moons in *complementary, but different elements,* such as fire with air and earth with water, won't have instant communication, but bonds are easily formed after you get to know each other.

The emotional challenges come when you blend two moons of *contrasting* elements, such as fire with earth or water, or air with earth or water. The success here depends on how many other planets are in harmony in your horoscopes, because on the emotional level, you will not instinctively communicate or understand each other. You'll have to work at it, make many compromises and adjustments.

Venus: What Turns You On

(You'll find your Venus placement and that of your partner in the tables on page 72.)

Your Venus placement reveals your tastes, what you respond to—very important things to consider when you're planning to live with someone. Look to Venus when you want to know what really pleases your partner or what your partner will *re*act to. Here again, the *element* of Venus should give you the key clues:

Venus in an earth sign responds to sensual and physical stimulation. This is a "material" girl or boy to whom comfortable physical surroundings, secure position and status are important. And this is a person who loves to touch and be touched (even though, with Venus in Virgo, the physical surroundings have to be "just so" before they warm up); so cuddle away!

Venus in an air sign will respond to an idea or an ideal. This is the girl (or boy) who "wants to have fun," can't stand to be bored. This person may have an ideal partner in mind, in terms of looks or personality. And he or she may have trouble finding the real counterpart. Companionship and friendship are often more important than physical attraction.

Venus in a fire sign responds to excitement, thrills, a good chase. Competition and challenges are sexy to them. Often the battle of the sexes is encouraged for that reason!

Venus in a water sign wants romance and responds to expressions of feelings. These people are very sentimental and need showers of affection, so don't hold back. Coolness is devastating to them. They love to give love.

Mars: What You Do to Others
(Look up the location of Mars in the tables on page 78.)

Mars is what you actively do to others. In a relationship, it shows how you make love or war, your temper, your manipulative style, what you do to get what you want—all very useful things to know about yourself and a potential partner!

Those with Mars in an earth sign make sensual physical love, with great stamina, though less finesse, than other signs. They may have naughty erotic fantasies under a conservative exterior style. When angered, these people react in several ways: They might dig in their heels stubbornly and not give an inch, or withdraw their support or knock out *your* support by incessant nagging or criticism.

Mars in an air sign plays head games. Here is the master of the scathing remark who plays it cool and often plays around. Angry displays cause them to breeze off or freeze any physical displays of affection. Confrontations and displays of passion are not their style. They'd prefer an elegant verbal duel.

Mars in a fire sign has the hottest temper. Everything is up front and out in the open with these people. You know where you stand. To win, they go in for bullying, open domination. Sexually it's all theatrical thrills—they like to be a bit daring and might even pick a battle of the sexes when things get dull. They love a good challenge and a good chase.

Mars in a water sign is the passive aggressor. The most negative types will whine, complain and feel very sorry for themselves. But they are never as helpless or victimized as they pretend, and Mars in Scorpio or Cancer can be very sneaky saboteurs. Water sign Mars people prefer emotional manipulation to open confrontation. But actively, they are romantic, emotional and sensitive lovers.

11

Career Counseling from the Stars

Can astrology direct you to a successful career? For many people, finding work that is productive and fulfilling both financially and creatively is a major goal. Whether you are just starting out, or thinking about a job change, or wondering if you made the right choice in the first place, your sun sign can give you some valuable clues about which way to turn.

Each sign has been observed to have its own approach to work and specific natural aptitudes that apply to the business world. Some signs, like Aries, are naturally more assertive; others, like Scorpio, are suited for wielding power behind the scenes; still others, like Leo, perform best in up-front, attention-getting positions. Here are their career characteristics, some jobs to consider and some stellar examples of sun sign tycoons.

Aries
This sign works well under pressure, loves an exciting, competitive, fast-paced atmosphere or a job that requires plenty of movement. You do not like to be trapped behind a desk, or tied down by strict regimentation. The more independence, the better. Aries Baron Phillipe de Rothschild of the famed banking family

found success on his own by developing "Mouton Roth-schild" wine (Note: *mouton* means ram, the symbol of Aries). You bring energy, enthusiasm and courage to the work place. However, you do not usually bring patience, tact and diplomacy. Bear this in mind when choosing your career.

Your best jobs: Anything involving pioneer work, sales, starting a new business, driving, engineering, fire fighting, the military, inventing, sports or physical education, maintenance of machinery, restaurant work (involving heat), manufacturing or selling trendy clothing or headgear.

Taurus

You are known for shrewd business sense. You like a safe business with solid financial backing and minimal risks. You're a slow but thorough worker who always finishes the job and is capable of building a substantial empire, like Taurean newspaper magnate William Randolph Hearst. Your Venusian love of beautiful tangible things and possible musical talent point to other good career directions.

Your best jobs: Real estate, banking, farming, construction work, anything in the music business (singer, musician, teacher), jewelry designer or gem trader, plants or flowers design.

Gemini

Tenants of this sign have strong communications skills. You think fast, expressing yourself easily, both verbally and in writing. Solitary work is not for you; you need to be around people. Neither is work that keeps you glued to one place or requires intense concentration. You are prone to change your job, if not your profession, several times. But you adapt easily and learn quickly. You also have great manual dexterity and like to keep your hands in motion. Cornelius Vanderbilt and Daniel Ludwig were quick-thinking, versatile Geminis who had the midas touch.

Your best jobs: Anything involving writing, selling, traveling, working with communications equipment (lots of telephones), journalism, publicity, hosting or hostessing at a restaurant.

Cancer

You can use your instinct for what people need—and will buy—with great success in business. You are one of the great money-earning signs of the zodiac as John D. Rockefeller and P. T. Barnum demonstrated. Providing for others' needs, whether it be banking services, shelter, food, fuel or home furnishings is your forte. Working on or with water would also be naturally congenial to you.

Your best jobs: Banking, shipping or selling boats, anything to do with restaurants, food retailing, catering, cooking, day care or nursery services, restoring or selling antiques, photography.

Leo

The lion needs to shine in business. You need a job that brings you the right kind of attention. In return, you are loyal, dedicated, and work with stamina as well as charisma. You need comfortable, if not luxurious, surroundings, hopefully in a prestige location. A natural boss, you prefer to delegate jobs than take orders yourself. You might enjoy running your own business, as does Malcolm Forbes, one of the world's most flamboyant tycoons.

Your best jobs: Selling or producing such status products as fine cars, jewelry, clothing; show business; party planning; hair styling or operating a beauty salon; host or hostessing at an elite restaurant or night club; publicity; heart surgery.

Virgo

People of this sign have a great capacity for organizing detailed jobs. Your critical ability can be productive in business where you're a stickler for quality control. Work requiring impeccable neatness, attention to detail, accuracy and methodical procedures is where you shine. You're especially keen when it comes to checking the work of others. Your talents are needed to provide the organization for a creative business, like publishing's Alfred Knopf.

Your best jobs: Anything in the health field from health food retailing to all forms of traditional and nontraditional medicine. Editing, education (you're a natural teacher), inspecting, quality control, printing, tailoring, producing films, technical or nonfiction writing, statistics, accounting. You also make an excellent industrial or graphic designer.

Libra

Here is a natural diplomat and negotiator. Your ability to weigh standards of fairness and beauty usually leads you into an artistic, academic or legal profession, like Charles Revson, founder of Revlon, or William Paley of C.B.S. Your cultivated artistic sense touches everything you do and can be channeled into money-making ventures. You should look for harmonious surroundings with compatible coworkers or a place where your diplomacy is much appreciated.

Your best jobs: Anything involving the arts, education, law, diplomacy. Or fashion, cosmetics, interior design, modeling, public relations. Jobs that keep the body in balance, such as chiropractic or nutrition planning, are other possibilities.

Scorpio

These people can see through to the core of a situation fast. With great drive and capacity for hard work you break through all obstacles to success. You are not afraid to take on responsibility or to take a chance. And you keep a cool head in a crisis. You function well in a structured organization where you can exercise power over others. You need to be in control of your surroundings and to find an outlet for your intense energies, like television's *l'enfant terrible,* Ted Turner.

Your best jobs: Medicine (some of the most noted surgeons, like Dr. Christiaan Barnard, are Scorpios), research, investigative work of all kinds, troubleshooting, locksmithing, police work, psychology, magic, tax collecting, mortuary work, or sex therapy. Work with fur or leather are other Scorpio fields.

Sagittarius

Your business assets include enthusiasm, optimism and a winning personality. You project a cheerful, positive mental attitude, and no one exemplified this better than Micky Mouse, created by Sagittarian Walt Disney. You are best in a job that requires movement, plenty of travel and public contact. Like billionaire oilman Jean Paul Getty, who made a fortune in Saudi Arabia, you may find success in a foreign country. You have great powers of persuasion and a spirit of adventure. You are best in risk-taking business that won't tie you down. Or you could be drawn to educational and religious institutions, or to supporting them, like Sagittarian philanthropist Andrew Carnegie.

Your best jobs: Publishing, sales, travel, import/export, religion and education-related work, professional sports or sports instruction, fashion retailing, outdoor work, anything involving animals, particularly horses.

Capricorns

These people are ambitious and well organized and take work very seriously, as did Howard Hughes and Aristotle Onassis. You'll work overtime, if it impresses higher-ups. You're quick to sense the power structure of any job situation—and make your plans accordingly. You usually stick to the tried and true and prefer a conservative firm, with status clients, though you can go it alone with great success. You're constantly improving yourself to better your chances.

Your best jobs: Corporate management, politics, corporate law, civil service, professors, status retailers, entrepreneurial ventures, pottery, sculpture, antiques, stained glass, ballet dancing or choreography.

Aquarius

Tenants of this sign can go either far out or very conservative in business and sometimes both at the same time, like Aquarian megatycoon H. L. Hunt, who wrote a utopian novel and campaigned for the most conservative causes. Aquarian inventiveness is best utilized in a free, open atmosphere, where you are interested in the job for its own sake. The key to your success: The job must engage you mentally. Sometimes you will work oblivious of financial reward. But a job that has a fair measure of public attention is sure to attract you.

Your best jobs: Counseling, psychology, scientific research, work with computers, radio, television, electrical energy, politics, work for an idealistic organization or charity, union work, anthropology, New Age therapies, yoga instruction, fund raising.

Pisces

This individual is exceptionally sensitive and intuitive, qualities which work wonders in many professions. Publishing's Rupert Murdoch and John Fairchild make productive use of their sixth sense, approaching their fast-paced, changeable businesses creatively. Pisces also needs freedom; you work best in an unstructured environment where there is an outlet for your active imagination and where you are surrounded by caring co-workers who build your confidence. Stay away from routine jobs, restrictive atmospheres and office politics.

Your best jobs: All the creative fields, the footwear or hosiery business, fishing or water-related businesses, fast-moving financial work, creative entrepreneureal ventures, politics, nursing, therapy. Cosmetics, oil and perfume, dance, anything to do with film, podiatry, reflexology.

Evaluating Your Success Potential

Many of us ponder whether we have what it takes to get to the top of our field or if we're destined to stay at the lower or middle management level. Several research studies have evaluated what talents or abilities make the difference between a moderate and an outstanding success. The findings prove that there are central skills and qualities involved—and it should be no surprise to the student of astrology that they can be traced to each of the signs. Since we're actually a combination of signs, considering all the planets in our horoscope, you're sure to have many of the top twelve qualities.

1. You can understand the underlying motives and desires of others, no matter what is happening on the surface.

Water signs Pisces, Cancer and Scorpio do this best.

2. You have an innate sense of who the most important people are and where the power lies in any situation.

Pisces, Cancer, Scorpio, Capricorn, Taurus and Virgo ferret this out easily.

3. Your objectivity allows you to understand other points of view. You never let your feelings get in the way.

An attribute of Aquarius, Virgo, Libra, Gemini.

4. You're self-confident in social situations: no problem hobnobbing with bigwigs.

Leo, Libra, Gemini, Sagittarius are the zodiac charmers.

5. You have such inner security that you stay in control of any situation. You're unflappable.

So are most of the fixed signs: Aquarius, Taurus, Scorpio, Leo.

6. You can mobilize your skills, motivate others, take quick action when necessary.

The cardinal signs—Aries, Capricorn, Cancer—can do it.

7. You love power. You *need* it.

Leo, Scorpio, Aries, Aquarius, Cancer and Capricorn like to make 'em jump.

8. You can live with ongoing stress.

Gemini, Sagittarius, Pisces, Virgo like excitement.

9. You communicate easily.

Gemini, Libra, Aquarius, Sagittarius love to express themselves verbally and in writing.

10. You arbitrate with others, solve disputes.

Libra, Gemini, Pisces, Aquarius are zodiac peace-makers.

11. You have a great sense of humor.

Gemini, Sagittarius, Pisces, Taurus and Aquarius can make us smile.

12. You're a good negotiator.

Taurus, Capricorn, Virgo, Scorpio and Cancer drive a tough bargain.

12

Planetary Programming

Now that you know how the sun, moon and planets and their astrological aspects affect your life, you'll want to take advantage of the positive forces that come your way and prepare for the rough times as much as possible. Here's how to set up a plan of action to get the most out of the moon, mercury, mars and venus positions.

Planning Your Moves by the Moon

When we set up an astrological timetable, we must first consider the power of the moon, the fastest moving heavenly body. It changes zodiac signs every two or three days, touching every sign and every planet in the course of a month, combining its energies with theirs to influence our lives.

The moon's reflective power makes us most receptive to the activities favored by each sign it enters. For instance, when the moon is in a sociable, communicative sign like Gemini, Libra, Leo or Sagittarius, it's a good time to step out—others will be in a convivial mood. When the moon is in businesslike Virgo or

Capricorn, you'll feel like getting organized and tackling detailed or routine chores.

When the moon passes the location of a planet in your horoscope, you'll feel it in the corresponding area of your life, though only for a few moments. Perhaps you have already noticed that there are certain times of the month when you really feel inspired to do certain things and other days when you're just "not in the mood." By looking up the location of the moon, you'll be able to plan your activities accordingly; you'll go with the flow.

Phasing in, Phasing Out

It's a general rule in astrology that any activity has a better chance of success if you begin while the moon is waxing, or growing full. This is the time when energy is gathering. By the full moon, a project should be well under way. Full moon times, when tensions, excitement and metabolic rates are at their peak, are not auspicious for beginning anything. It's a better time to bring your plans to light, go public, show off. Wind down through the last quarter until the next new moon, when you'll get the green light to start again.

During the new moon: Get things going, try something new, meet a new lover, plant crops that grow above the ground.

During the first quarter: Search for lost articles, build on your projects, pursue your goals, begin a serious romance.

At the full moon: Harvest crops, get married, sell your ideas, act on an attraction to the opposite sex, but avoid arguments and avoid surgery.

At the last quarter: Break up a romance (you'll feel the least pain, now!), plant crops that grow below the ground. Rest, relax, reorganize and reevaluate.

The Go-Ahead Sign

When the moon is in your sun sign, you'll find things going your way effortlessly. It's easier to influence people positively. But when the moon is opposite your sun sign (six signs away), better lie low, relax and reflect.

You can follow the moon's changes, easily; they are listed with your daily forecasts in the back of the book. Note how the effort on your own moods and those of your friends and co-workers coincides with the following trends.

Moon in Aries

Go ahead: You'll feel a new surge of energy. It's a great day for activities that require competition, quick decisions. You're on the prowl for excitement and adventure. Hunting, speculating on stocks or real estate, cooking and getting a new haircut are favored. And it's a good time to do something you've never done before. Challenge yourself, now.

Hold back: People tend to be very impatient, quick tempered. You'll be intolerant of any delays or attempts to thwart your plans; you want to get your own way, immediately. Be careful not to step on any toes. And watch out for head injuries.

Moon in Taurus

Go ahead: Continue projects you started a few days ago or begin a long-term project. Enjoy sensual pleasures of all kinds. However, with an increased appetite for anything that feels, looks, smells or tastes good, you may find it difficult to stay on a diet. It's time to take necessary steps to protect your security, make long-range plans, dig new foundations or hold on to what you've got. Tackle a tough project that requires perseverance and concentration.

Hold back: Don't push today, you'll find people stubborn and resistant to change. And it's not a good day to get things done quickly. Slow and thorough are the keywords. If you gamble or speculate now, you may find decisions difficult to alter later. In love, casual flirtations will be taken seriously.

Moon in Gemini
Go ahead: This is a restless gadabout time when you'll want to get out and about, meet new people, get on the telephone. It's a better day for talk than action—ideal for meetings of all kinds, business and social. Short trips, letters, and tasks that require manual dexterity also flow smoothly.

Hold back: Keep it light today. And watch out for gossip; be especially discreet—you could spill the beans. People will talk now. Be careful when you make promises; you may change your mind later or not be able to deliver.

Moon in Cancer
Go ahead: This is the most emotional time of the month. Your heart rules your head, so act accordingly. It's time to pay attention to family needs; do some mothering or phone home. Do things that make others feel emotionally secure. Let your loved ones know how much you care. You may also get some intuitive flashes—your instincts are quite reliable now.

Hold back: Everyone is quite sensitive. Be careful not to hurt feelings; any criticism is taken to heart and people may respond irrationally to imagined slights. You may gain an extra pound or two, thanks to fluid retention or calorie laden "comfort" foods.

Moon in Leo
Go ahead: You'll want to be admired and adored today. People are thinking big; they're kind and generous. Now's the time to ask for a raise. To get favorable

attention, wear your most stunning outfit, some spectacular jewelry, an especially dramatic accessory. Make a big play for someone. You can sell today. Some other options: travel for pleasure, breaking a bad habit, a smashing new hairstyle, sending someone flowers.

Hold back: Save the budgeting till later, but be careful not to spend beyond your means. This is not the time for nit-picking. People are full of themselves—you'll look like a wet blanket. Watch out for scene stealers and bossy domineering types who demand attention.

Moon in Virgo
Go ahead: Take care of those details and tiresome chores that have been piling up. Do some constructive planning or reorganizing. Clean off your desk. Clean your closets. Get the job done. It's a good day for a checkup, a workout, a trip to the health food store. Or start a diet or an evening self-improvement course.

Hold back: Not the time for independent work, speculation, or asking for a raise. People are tight-fisted and eagle-eyed now. You'll be supercritical—keep it constructive.

Moon in Libra
Go ahead: Go out and socialize. This is the time for doing things in tandem. Form a partnership of any kind. Everyone feels more friendly, more tolerant, more diplomatic. There's an urge to beautify yourself and your surroundings. Buy a new outfit, go to the hair stylist, turn on the charm. You may have a romantic encounter, at least an enjoyable flirtation.

Hold back: It's not a great time for making definite decisions. You're still in the negotiating frame of mind. You may be feeling a bit lazy too, so don't undertake anything too physically strenuous. And it's the worst time for a heavy emotional discussion. Keep it light.

Moon in Scorpio

Go ahead: Now everyone is more intense. Some are downright passionate. If you're in love, this is a super-sexy time. Deep emotional interactions are favored. So are buying antiques, breaking off with someone permanently, seeing a psychic, doing investigative research. Your concentration is terrific; you can absorb yourself in a difficult job and make real progress.

Hold back: This is generally considered the worst time for surgery. Guard against jealousy and any extreme emotional reactions. People are quick to take offense. Be on guard for underhanded tactics. All may not be as it appears on the surface. Look behind the scenes.

Moon in Sagittarius

Go ahead: Now's the time to make a deal, get a loan, start off on a long trip. People are unusually good-humored. It's a great time for a party. You'll feel lots of confidence; you can really sell your ideas today. It's also a good time to deal with religious or educational institutions, with publishers or travel agents, or to give a lecture.

Hold back: You may feel like you're on a lucky roll. Don't get carried away. What is planned today may turn out to be a flight of fancy—more talk than action. It's not a good time for attending to details or practical matters. Or for sedentary shut-in activities.

Moon in Capricorn

Go ahead: Now's the time to buckle down, get organized. You can accomplish much. Plan how to utilize your assets to improve your station in life. Buy antiques, start a new job, do some shrewd speculating and attend to banking matters (but don't ask for a loan). There's an air of seriousness and purpose about everything you do. Attend to family duties, especially those involving elderly relatives.

Hold back: This is a rather stingy moon—not the time to ask for a loan or a raise. Concentrate on doing your job well. You'll be noticed later. There's also a tendency toward pessimism and depression. Guard against negativity. You'll kick up your heels another day.

Moon in Aquarius

Go ahead: You may find yourself dealing with the public today. At least you'll be contacting friends. It's time to think of the welfare of others, to meet in groups. It's a good time to experiment or try something new. You may suddenly feel the need for more freedom and want to break away from restrictions. A new course of study, joining a club or taking up a cause may satisfy your craving for novelty. You may be in for a surprise from out of the blue today.

Hold back: People are coolly objective today: it's not the time for sticky scenes; save your personal troubles for later. You may tend to idealize or rationalize your emotional situation. Watch out for shocks—electrical and otherwise.

Moon in Pisces

Go ahead: This is an emotional, rather solitary time good for intimate one-to-one dealings or even better, meditation and introspection. Others are feeling vulnerable, withdrawn, self-protective. It's a good time for soul-searching discussions over a good bottle of wine. Someone may feel like crying on your shoulder. If you're going out, try an artistic recreation—a new movie, dancing or listening to music. If you must take action, do something creative; you'll have insight and imagination.

Hold back: Steer clear of practical routines and active competition. People may play on your sympathies, undermine you emotionally. Because you're extra sensitive, sentimental and passive, you can be easily discouraged, especially by thoughtless words or criticism. Don't be a soft touch for a sob story.

Eclipses—Take "Time Out"

Eclipses of the sun and moon, when these powerful luminaries are literally blacked out, have always been ominous occurrences. These are times when confusion, instability and fruitless activity prevail. It's wise for you to take time out; do only what is absolutely necessary during the "shadow of the eclipse," ten days before and three days after. Though there may be a shake-up around you, try not to start anything; otherwise, expect the unexpected. This applies especially to Pisces and Virgo in 1988.

Eclipses in 1988:

Lunar: March 3 in Virgo
Solar: March 17 in Pisces
Lunar: August 27 in Pisces
Solar: September 10 in Virgo

Get the Mercury Message

During the times when Mercury is retrograde (appears to be moving backward in the sky), be prepared for difficulties in communications and don't sign anything. Expect important mail to be delayed, telephone messages to get confused or cut off, travel plans to take unexpected directions. Everything you do now will need adjustment later!

In 1988, Mercury goes retrograde three times. All take place when the planet is traveling through air signs, and since these signs are the communicators of the zodiac, they will be especially vulnerable. So Libras, Geminis, and Aquarians, take note of these days. Allow for delays, if not snafus, and keep your sense of humor!

1988 Mercury Retrograde Dates:

February 2–23 in Aquarius
May 31–June 24 in Gemini
September 28–October 20 in Libra

Mars and Your High Energy Times

When Mars is in your sun sign, you're energized, enthusiastic, maybe a bit hot-tempered. This is the time to go for whatever you want; be assertive. You can work long hours, tackle the tough jobs that require stamina and stand up for your rights. It's best for physical work where you can let off steam. But be careful not to get carried away and take needless risks. And be careful not to step on others' tender feelings. This is a time where you may leap before you look, disregarding the possible consequences of your actions. Stay out of arguments and use the energy positively.

Since the red planet takes two years to orbit the sun, six signs per year get the full whammy. In 1988, Mars changes signs on the following dates:

January 8: Mars moves into Sagittarius
February 22: into Capricorn
April 6: into Aquarius
May 22: into Pisces
July 13: into Aries
October 23: into Pisces
November 1: into Aries
These signs will have Mars energy this year!

143

When Venus Makes
Your Sex Appeal Soar

When Venus is in the same sign as your sun, get ready for love. Your magnetism will draw others to you. You'll be irresistible. You'll also be more creative and inspired by beautiful surroundings. It's time for pleasure all around—don't spoil it by working too hard.

In 1988, Venus will enter these lucky signs on the following dates:

January 15: Pisces
February 9: Aries
March 6: Taurus
April 3: Gemini
May 17: Cancer
May 27: Gemini
August 6: Cancer
September 7: Leo
October 4: Virgo
October 29: Libra
November 23: Scorpio
December 17: Sagittarius

Heed the Positions of All Four

Go-Ahead Dates

The moon placements in your daily forecast and the planetary timetables in this chapter will give you the exact dates.

• When the moon is in your sun sign.
• From the new moon till the time the moon is full.
• When Mercury is direct.
• When Venus is in your sun sign.
• When Mars is in your sun sign.

When to Hold Back and Center Yourself
• Ten days preceding and three days following an eclipse of the sun or moon.
• Moon in the opposite sign (six signs away) from your sun.
• Moon waning from the full moon to the new moon.
• Mercury retrograde
• Venus or Mars three or six signs away from your sun sign.

Timing Your Career
• Ask for a raise: moon in Leo or Sagittarius.
• Start a new project: moon in Aries, Sagittarius, Capricorn, new moon, first and second quarters.
• Stay with your job, when the going's rough: eclipses; Mercury retrogrades; moon in Taurus, Leo, Aquarius, Scorpio.
• Quit a job: moon in Gemini, Virgo, Sagittarius; moon in the last quarter; Mars in your sun sign.
• Look for a new job: moon in Aries, Sagittarius, Gemini or Libra.
• Sign a firm agreement: moon in Taurus, Mercury direct, moon in first quarter.
• Sue!: Mars in Aries.
• Invest in the stock market: The market tends to be low at the new and full moon, higher 8 to 10 days before or 8 to 10 days after the new moon.

Your Health
• Unfavorable times for surgery: moon in Scorpio or Aries, full moon or when the moon is in the sign ruling the part of the body to be operated on. Or if the moon is in the square or opposition aspect (three or six signs away) to Mars.
• Best time for surgery: first week after the new moon, if it is not in the same sign as your sun and meets the above conditions.

- Best time for plastic surgery: moon in Libra or Leo.
- Best time for a checkup: moon in Virgo.
- Dental work: moon in Capricorn.

Your Love Life

- Meet a new lover: at the new moon, or when Venus or Mars is in your sun sign.
- Socialize: Moon in Aquarius, Gemini, Leo, Libra, Sagittarius.
- You're at your most attractive when: Venus is in your sun sign.
- Propose when: Mercury is direct, moon is waxing.
- Break off when: moon is waning, last quarter.
- Get married when: moon is full.
- Get divorced: last quarter moon.

13

Exercise and Diet with Your Sign

According to ancient astrological tradition, each sign governs an area of the body or one of its regulatory systems. These areas are your special sensitive spots, depending on your sign, and must be emphasized in the way you maintain and use your body. When strengthened, your sun sign area can be a tremendous asset to you. Many dancers were born under Pisces, which rules the feet. Many skiers and runners are Sagittarians, which rules the upper leg. When abused, however, these areas become your weak points. Leo is especially vulnerable to heart disease and Aries to head injuries (it is said that most Arians have a scar on their face or head). So pay attention to these parts and systems of your body, when planning your health, exercise, diet and beauty care.

ARIES rules the head and brain, the red blood cells.

TAURUS rules the throat and thyroid gland.

GEMINI rules the nervous system, lungs and the shoulders, arms and hands.

CANCER rules the digestive system, breasts and sinus cavities and membranes.

LEO rules the heart and spinal vertebrae.

VIRGO rules the pancreas, spleen and intestinal tract.

LIBRA rules the kidneys, lower back and basal metabolism.

SCORPIO rules the reproductive and lower eliminative system.

SAGITTARIUS rules the hips, thighs and buttocks muscles, the sciatic nerve and the carbon dioxide elimination of the lungs.

CAPRICORN rules the teeth, bones, knees and gallbladder.

AQUARIUS rules the ankles, the blood circulation system and the spinal cord.

PISCES rules the feet and the lymphatic system.

Astro-Athletics—
How Your Sun Sign Scores

In the overall umbrella of your sun sign, there are many qualities that could help you become a top athlete. Though there is no one sign for each sport—you'll find great tennis stars born under Pisces (Ivan Lendl), Virgo (Jimmy Connors), Libra (Martina Navratilova), for instance—you'll find that each sign has certain qualities that can be used to give the player a competitive edge. The perfectionism of Virgo, the balance of Libra, the sensitivity and sixth sense of Pisces give each of the players mentioned unique advantages—so can the strengths of your sign help *you* win points!

Your sun sign will give you insight, not only into the kind of activity that might appeal to you, but also the best way to approach it. If you should go for a solitary sport or one where you train with others. If you are suited for an artistic activity like ice skating or a competitive sport like marathon running. You'll also learn about your body's weak point, so you can protect and strengthen that area.

Aries

This person has great speed, drive, coordination and a love of winning. In fact, competition is essential to bringing out your best. You really shine in crowd-pleasing team sports that demand split-second decisions like basketball (Kareem Abdul-Jabbar and Walt Frazier) and baseball (Pete Rose). You are especially vulnerable to head injuries, so remember to wear protective headgear. Mars-ruled Arians could also take out their aggressive streak in martial arts, track, downhill racing or, just for fun, tap dancing. Activities that provide lots of stimulation and excitement will hold your interest. Those that require patience or long training periods are not for you.

Taurus

Tenants of this sign have great stamina, concentration and the patience necessary to wait for the optimum moment and to endure long, arduous training. Boxers Joe Louis, Gene Tunney and Sugar Ray Robinson, tennis star Pancho Gonzales, baseball's Yogi Berra and Willie Mays and gymnast Olga Korbut prove it. But, because you prefer a soft, comfortable life-style, you can easily put on weight. It takes a new love interest to get you back in shape fast. Find a way to make workouts sensually pleasurable. Jogging in a beautiful park or woodland or exercising to your favorite music will help. Your natural sense of rhythm could attract you to aerobics, roller and ice skating and dance (like Fred Astaire). Pay special attention to your neck, Taurus's vulnerable area; you may hold tension there. Try pressure point massage to relieve kinks and stress.

Gemini

These athletes have great manual dexterity, intelligence, quick wits, good timing and versatility—which give them an extra edge in competition. Joe Namath, Jim Thorpe,

Lou Gehrig, Wilma Rudolph, Johnny Weissmuller, Bjorn Borg and Sam Snead are prime examples. Your restlessness and wonderful co-ordination work for you in speed sports. You prefer exercise that involves others, that is a form of social activity and that has enough variety to sustain your interest. Since Gemini is associated with the arms, lungs and hands, these are the special areas vulnerable to injury. Aerobic exercises for lung conditioning should be part of your daily routine. Yoga is also valuable for its deep breathing techniques and its calming, centering effect on jangled Gemini nerves.

Cancer

Your sports ability centers around your intuitive sense. Uncannily, you seem to know what your opponent is going to do in advance. O. J. Simpson, Arthur Ashe and Ilie Nastase bring Cancerian creativity to their sport. In tense competitive situations, you may be vulnerable to an upset stomach. Spend some time each day working off stress with an enjoyable, noncompetitive activity like walking or swimming. Burn off extra calories with solitary rope skipping, cycling or one-on-one training sessions. Sports performed on the water, especially anything to do with boats, come naturally to you.

Leo

You may be slow to get started on an exercise routine, but you'll be more motivated if there's a glamorous end in sight, like a sleek new dress to wear, or an actual performance where you'll steal the show. Performing before admiring crowds is an aphrodisiac to you. The bigger the crowd, the more important the event, the better. Esther Williams, Peggy Fleming, Renee Richards, Rafer Johnson (decathlon), Vitas Gerulaitis, Evonne Goolagong Cawley and Rod Laver (tennis), Willy Shoemaker (jockey), and Wilt Chamberlain know how to grab the big sports spotlight. Once you're focused on a sport where you can shine, you'll work at it without ceasing. Look for some great workout clothes since you like to be a star at all times. A luxurious health club is a great place to get moving in style. You should include aerobic conditioning to strengthen your heart—Leo's most vulnerable point.

Virgo

This sign's athletes push themselves to achieve perfection, are never satisfied with their performance. Football's Terry Bradshaw, golf's Arnold Palmer, tennis's Jimmy Connors, and skiing's Jean-Claude Killy are prime examples. But your incessant self-criticism and the tension it provokes, both within you and in others, can boomerang, upsetting your digestion and causing extreme nervous tension. Find solace in relaxing hatha yoga, like Raquel Welch, or in solitary activities like gardening. Make exercise a natural part of your daily routine; walking or cycling to work, lunch hour exercise breaks or gentle stretching during the day will improve your efficiency. And be sure your working environment is conducive to physical fitness. A chair with good back support, a source of fresh air and good lighting will cut down on possible sources of irritation.

Libra

Your greatest asset in sports is your sense of balance. You know how to pace yourself, when not to overexert. Phil Rizzuto, Dave DeBusschere (basketball), Martina Navratilova and Sheila Young (speed skater) are among your sign's star athletes. You prefer social sports where you join others. Dancing, bicycling, fencing and tennis are naturals. You like to exercise in a harmonious environment and, even though you're usually able to detach yourself mentally from the more hysterical side of competition, you'll find that any extreme situations in your emotional life have an adverse effect on your performance. Be sure to protect and strengthen your lower back—your most vulnerable area.

Scorpio
Single-minded intensity and drive are your best assets in competitive sports. You'll fight for your goal no matter what, never giving up. The roughest training won't faze you. There are many star athletes born under Scorpio like Pele (soccer), Bruce Jenner, Billie Jean King, Nadia Comeneci, Tom Seaver, Whitey Ford (pitcher), Frank Shorter (running). You are particularly suited to demanding solitary sports like gymnastics and the triathalon. You like a challenge and the bigger, the better. Martial arts, body-building, surfing and scuba diving, as well as competition swimming are terrific. Compulsive training, however, can have negative effects. Be sure to pace yourself, balancing your activity with enough relaxation.

Sagittarius
These are natural athletes, seemingly born in motion. You excel in sports that require strong thigh muscles like racewalking, running, skiing and especially horseback riding, including polo, jumping and racing. Suzy Chaffee, Chris Evert Lloyd, Joe DiMaggio and Stan Musial are among the many Sag sports stars. Jane Fonda's workout tapes could be the answer to exercising when you travel. Just take your classes along with you. Your on-the-go life-style itself is a form of exercise. Try to stay in hotels that have a fitness center or pool where you can work out or keep a diary of exercise classes and health clubs that offer one-time visits in the cities on your itinerary. And be sure to pack running shoes, leotard and sweat suit, always!

Capricorn

This sign's individuals have the natural discipline to make a great athlete like Muhammed Ali and golfer Nancy Lopez. Ballet, which requires intense dedication, has many Capricorn stars, like Gelsey Kirkland. Your knees are very vulnerable, so be sure to protect them. Joining an exclusive health club or tennis or country club has double appeal for you—the chance to make business contacts while you enjoy a sport or workout. Be sure to take full advantage of any sports activities your business provides: company gyms and exercise classes, squash courts, running tracks. You do need to exercise, even though you may be naturally slender, to work off job stresses.

Aquarius

Your sign rules the calves and ankles, so your sport should involve activity in that area. Tennis's John MacEnroe, baseball's Hank Aaron, golf's Jack Nicklaus and swimming's Mark Spitz are Aquarian champions. You love working out with gadgets, like weights and exercise machines. You may prefer to exercise at odd hours, so an at-home gym is a good idea. You may prefer to combine your exercise with a form of meditation, like the Tai Chi or yoga. Or you could make up an exercise routine of your own using videotapes of your favorite televised classes. You have a mind of your own, don't care about pleasing the masses (though you often do, anyway) and approach your form of exercise in a unique way.

Pisces

The extreme sensitivity possessed by Pisceans may appear to be a liability in the rough and tumble world of sports, but if used properly, it can be a tremendous advantage. Grand Prix race drivers Mario Andretti, Janet Guthrie, Johnny Rutherford and Bobby Unser team their own split-second timing with the world's most sensitive machines. Baseball's Pete Rozell and hockey's Bobby Orr are other examples. This sign which rules the feet has naturally produced the footwork of ballet's Rudolf Nureyev and Fernando Bujones. You'll approach any sport with creativity and imagination, however you may shy away from competitive sports, preferring more solitary activities that bring you closer to nature—preferably the sea—lift away blue moods and work off tension. Since your feet are vulnerable to injury, be sure to get the proper shoes for your particular sport; have them custom-fitted if necessary.

Diet Do's and Don't s

Since astrology has so many correlations, it should come as no surprise that our attitudes toward food and diet are related to our sun signs. Whether you pile on pounds slowly or balloon rapidly, respond to a disciplined diet or rebel against any routine, or have the willpower to eat in gourmet restaurants or must stick to salad bars—many of the secrets to shedding weight are here in the stars. Use them to work out a diet plan that is harmonious to your basic nature.

Aries—The Energy Burner

You need lots of the right kind of fuel for your active life. You're impatient with slow mealtimes, and though you love good food, you often pay little attention to what you eat in your haste to pursue other activities. In dieting, you're impetuous. You'll try the latest fad diet for instant results, then get furious if the pounds don't drop off. You may forget food entirely, then binge. To avoid energy burnout, it's important for you to develop healthy food habits. Frequent small meals of fruits, vegetables and lean meat may be best for you, but stay away from fast-food stands. If spicy, ethnic food attracts you (your sign rules garlic and ginger, also peppers of all kinds), invent your own low-calorie versions of Mexican, Indian or Chinese favorites.

Taurus—Those Taste Sensations

Food is a sensual experience for Taureans. You thoroughly enjoy the smell, texture and visual beauty of food as well as the taste. The act of chewing and savoring food is also part of the pleasure, one in which you like to indulge as often as possible. You'll put off starting a diet indefinitely, and it is particularly difficult for your sign to stick to a diet. One diet turn-off is monotony. Another is bland tastes. Your best bet is to find a diet that has visual and taste appeal. And one that allows you enough food—big salads of the most beautiful fruits and vegetables, baked potato (skip the butter), popcorn. Bring out your best china, crystal, silver and add fresh flowers to give yourself sumptuous surroundings, so you won't feel deprived.

Gemini—The Social Eater

To keep you from getting easily bored, you need a diet that has variety. You are too busy to worry about food, often eat under pressure or may eat while doing something else—like talking on the telephone or watching television. In fact, you may be so engrossed in activity that you eat anything at hand and that's when the calories pile on. You may also eat many meals in restaurants, where you like to sample everything on the table. That's why you love buffets, where there is a great selection of food. Try satisfying your need for variety by composing a meal of appetizers. Or try an exotic cuisine, like Japanese, which is also nonfattening. Keep healthy finger food to "graze" on. You love good conversation during a meal, but remember to chew your food thoroughly and let your dinner companions expound. Choose foods that are easy to digest if you've been under too much stress lately.

Cancer—Eating for Comfort

You're a moody, emotional eater who is especially sensitive to the atmosphere of the meal. Tension can easily give you indigestion. You appreciate fine gourmet cuisine and the wines which accompany it, as well as the warmth of big family meals together—particularly if you're the chef, using grandmother's recipes for rich calorie-laden sauces and desserts. You may stick to your "favorite" comfort foods, rather than experiment with exotic recipes, which may be difficult to digest. You tend to retain water and can balloon up and down in cycles. Eat seafood, rather bland cream sauces; delicate foods soothe you but watch alcohol intake, salt and diuretics. Instead, try a diet day of fruit and vegetable juices or slim down on fresh fish and vegetables.

Leo—The Royal Repast

Leo meals should be fit for a king, perhaps accompanied by champagne and a grande finale dessert like cherries jubilee. You love to be the gracious host or hostess entertaining friends at a lavish restaurant, a glamorous social occasion or a big dinner party, sparing no expense to treat your guests to the finest. You're probably a regular at the best restaurants in town. You should watch your cholesterol level—you're prone to heart problems and very fond of filet mignon. Learn to make wise choices at the buffet table. Resist rich foods but not rich table settings. Nothing that makes you feel poor or deprived will hold you for long. So make your diet meals as much of an event as your banquets. You may consider taking your next vacation at a pampering spa, where you're treated like royalty while you shed those extra pounds.

Virgo—Eating Healthy

You are so health- and diet-conscious that you feel guilty when you add the least bit of extra weight. Chances are, you've studied nutrition on your own and are no stranger to the health food stores. You'll stick to a diet that is medically approved, with plenty of whole grains, unrefined foods, fresh fruits and veggies that you can fit into your daily routine. You're another one with a nervous stomach, so food should be easily digestible. If you're gaining, make a food chart recording what you eat every day for two weeks; then you'll be able to zero in on the culprit—be it a bad habit, too many cocktail parties, too much bread with meals, or nervous munchies.

Libra—Glorious Goodies

You like food that is beautifully presented, preferably in a social setting. Glorious desserts can be your downfall since your sign usually has a sweet tooth. Let your intinctive sense of balance work for you. When you've had too much of any one thing, your body feels out of sorts. You could create beautiful desserts of fruits and low-calorie fillings that are edible works of art. You'll stick to a diet if you have company. Join a diet group or find a friend to share dieting with and check up on each other. An appeal to your vanity will often set you off on a crash regimen. Instead, plan a sensible diet and buy a beautiful new outfit—a trifle too small. Then, when the new clothes fit perfectly, plan a night on the town to wear them.

Scorpio—Strong Appetites

Scorpio does everything to extremes; that includes eating and dieting. Once you make up your mind to shed pounds, nothing can deter you. You'll literally starve yourself to get them off fast. You're a binger who overindulges in your favorite treats, then feels guilty and crash diets later. This can set up a very unhealthy seesaw tendency. You can also overindulge in alcohol, which will throw your system off balance. Mushrooms, licorice, sushi, lots of garlic and spices and dark whole grain bread are Scorpio delights. Challenge yourself to get your system in harmony with a diet of fresh raw foods; the fiber and natural roughage will cleanse your body of toxins. However, any diet efforts should be dedicated to establishing good food habits, not just a crash-binge alternative. Try to find other outlets to absorb your energies—a new hobby, an adult education course or vigorous exercise.

Sagittarius—Eating on the Run

Your active life-style keeps you in shape, but your love of exotic foods and your constant travel may set up rushed eating habits, a craving for junk foods for instant energy and overindulging when you do sit down for a meal. It is very difficult for you to settle down to any diet routine. To combat this, your dieting should allow for your travel schedule in working in fresh, wholesome food, so you won't be tempted by fast meals on the road. Liquid breakfasts whipped up in a blender with ingredients like fruit juice, protein powder, yogurt, brewer's yeast are good meals on the run. Stock up in trail mix, nuts, dried fruits and quick energy snacks and avoid caffeine and soft drinks. Or carry some wholesome munchies with you.

Capricorn—The Disciplined Dieter

You take your nutrition seriously. Chances are, you've organized your mealtimes well and you'll stick to any diet you start if it is sensible—no extreme fasts or pineapple diets for you. You want long-lasting results. The problem usually comes with working too hard to get enough exercise or those incessant business lunches and dinners. Status restaurants can be another diet downfall. Make a list before you go shopping; don't waver from it. Set diet goals and give yourself rewards for achieving them. One svelte Capricorn gives herself points for each time she passes up a high-calorie temptation then pays herself off with a non-food prize like a manicure or massage.

Aquarius—The Food Faddist

Computer diets, biofeedback training, vegetarian guru diets—anything new, experimental or unusual in food fascinates you. A craving for salty foods or airy foods like whipped cream, soufflés, puff pastry could be your nemesis. But, you'll stick with a diet that you find interesting intellectually. It should have some strong overall theory or idealistic context—consisting of unrefined, organically pure unpolluted foods, for instance. Or it should be presented in an interesting, maybe exotic way such as eating with chopsticks to force yourself to take smaller portions. You have to believe in the diet to stay with it for any length of time. A vacation at a yoga retreat may get you back on the track if irregular eating habits have caught up with you.

Pisces—Those Hungry Feelings

Pisces are emotional eaters, who eat—or drink—for comfort, then pile on the pounds. Any emotional stimulus can trigger an eating spree. You may also tend to snack in between meals rather than binge, creating a constant flow of food. Liquid retention is another problem. Try natural diuretic teas, drink a lot of water in addition to other liquids. Stay away from stimulants or depressants—caffeine or alcohol, with its hidden calories. Your system is very sensitive. You'll stick to a diet that satisfies you emotionally. So be sure that it includes at least one favorite comfort food, some fresh seafood, and is eaten in a tranquil, loving atmosphere. Watch the times you eat, don't eat when upset. It's a much better idea to take a walk or exercise until your mood changes. Liquid meals of fruit and vegetable juices will rest and cleanse your system. You are also influenced by what others around you are eating. Cultivate some skinny friends and avoid big family meals if possible while you are dieting. Eating a small meal before you socialize could keep you from gorging at the buffet.

14

Sun Sign Fashion and Beauty Tips

The rays of your sun sign, which touch all areas of your life, are also reflected in how you choose to appear to the world. Each sign has certain physical features and special attitudes that can express your best feelings about yourself. Here's how to take advantage of your sun sign charisma.

Aries—Energy and Sparkle

You're a leader in fashion, and, like Diana Ross or Paloma Picasso, sure to be noticed and imitated. You love to be the first on the block with the newest look. By the time others have copied you, you're on to the next hot new item. Since Aries rules the head, you should pay special attention to your hair style. Get the best haircut in town and keep it shining. You look wonderful in hats—the more dramatic, the better. Be sure to play up your distinctive eyebrows and well-shaped forehead. You can use bold, daring touches with great style. Interpretations of the military uniforms look wonderful on you; so bring on the bomber jackets, epaulets and trench coats. Like Joan Crawford, you may be the perfect foil for master-tailoring and dramatic forceful lines. Always wear a bit of red somewhere!

Taurus—Sensual Style

You find the most comfortable style and stick to it, whether you're as classic as Candice Bergen or as flamboyant as Cher. You're best in a simple, but sensual look, executed in luxurious tactile fabrics. Play up your femininity with perfume and precious or semiprecious jewelry. Your hair should look touchable, whether its softly waving or a mass of curls. Show off your beautiful neckline with off-the-shoulder styles, a striking necklace. Your Taurus colors are greens and soft floral shades.

Gemini—Playful and Witty

You enjoy fashion, but don't take it too seriously. From the sexiness of Joan Collins or the outrageousness of Cindy Lauper to the glowing youth of Brooke Shields, you use clothes to communicate the many different sides of your personality. Light colors and airy fabrics suit you. Always tuned in to fashion news, you can use accessories to instantly transform a basic outfit into a variety of looks. Keep your expensive hands beautifully manicured and adorned with striking rings. You need a versatile haircut or a basic style that you can wear many diferent ways. You may also consider streaked hair or a shading of light color around your face. Lemon yellow, airy blue or silver-grey express your mercurial nature.

Cancer—Always Feminine

No matter what you wear, even blue jeans and combat boots, you project femininity. Most of you have innate good taste, exemplified by Diahann Carroll, Princess Diana and Nancy Reagan, and intuitively understand the appropriate look for every occasion. You look best in soft, romantic but elegant clothes, and beautifully coiffed, wavy hair. You have a luminous quality at night, and often look your best in evening wear. Soft, subdued shades, lunar white and navy are your special colors. Pearls and silver suit you better than flashy jewels. You may have very sensitive skin; moon maidens don't always respond to sunlight. Be sure to play up your beautiful eyes with discreet makeup.

Leo—Star Quality
Madonna, Jacqueline Onassis and Linda Carter have the kind of big-time beauty and poise that steals spotlights. The trick here is not to overdo. Take a lesson from Yves St. Laurent, a Leo fashion designer who creates spectacular but tasteful effects. Leo is one sign that can wear lots of jewelry, real or pretend; after all, your color is gold. You should pay special attention to your hair—it should always be a gorgeous mane—and your radiant Miss America smile.

Virgo—Clean and Natural
Clothes must be functional and comfortable as well as good-looking for Virgo. Watch a tendency to look too prim. You dislike clutter, too many accessories. Clean-lined, well-designed looks in natural fibers are best for you. You can be uncompromising about fit and fabric. Like Ingrid Bergman or Lauren Bacall, you may prefer classic styles. Or you could play up your earthiness and great physical shape, like Sophia Loren or Raquel Welch. You look best in carefully-thought-out makeup—nothing too wild or experimental. Your astrological colors are clear blue, the pale earthy wheat colors, crisp white.

Libra—A Sense of Proportion
Your eye for balance and harmony has always made you one of fashion's darlings, though you rarely go for extreme shapes or colors. Anything off balance makes you very uncomfortable; that's why you'll spend hours shopping for just the right shoe or the perfect coat. Like Catherine Deneuve, you could solve your problem

by sticking to one favorite designer, or like Cheryl Tiegs, by designing your own clothes. You know instinctively how to play up your best features with different accessories and color combinations. A soft, slightly wavy hairstyle enhances your classic features. You may favor pastels, particularly pink. You need little makeup, just enough to define your eyes and cupid-bow lips.

Scorpio—A Powerful Presence

You make a strong, unwavering statement—either cool and classic like Jaclyn Smith and Linda Evans or vibrant and dramatic like Vivien Leigh. You may like to underplay your sexiness by wearing rather severe, menswear-influenced styles. Designers like Calvin Klein understand your love of uncluttered, classic sportswear. Use makeup to play up your intense eyes and beautiful cheekbones, and pay extra attention to skin care. You love to get suntans and may pay the price in damaged skin later. You wear black, particularly black leather, like no one else. Scorpio blondes also look best in icy pales.

Sagittarius—Fashion Freedom

You love trendy fashion and wear it with definite flair. There's nothing wishy-washy about the clothes or colors you choose, or the way you wear them. You're an eye-catcher, whether exotic and avante garde like Tina Turner or fresh and natural like Liv Ullmann. Usually you prefer the outdoor look in clothes that move easily with your active body (nothing confining, ever). Get an easy-care hairstyle that adapts to your hectic life. You may need extra conditioning to keep it looking good after lots of sun exposure. And play up those great legs—with tennis or running shorts, short skirts, slit skirts, great stockings, beautiful shoes. Purple, orange and turquoise are your special colors.

Capricorn—The Realist

You have an eye for quality designer clothes, in styles that you can wear for years, and that whisper of money and status. Capricorn designer Diane Von Furstenburg has your message. Versatile separates that can mix, match and really stretch a wardrobe are your best investment. So are accessories from the best boutiques, and by all means, a beautiful fur. Your sign bestows great bone structure—the kind that ages best, as Marlene Dietrich, Faye Dunaway and Susan Lucci display. You need hair that looks great at the office, can turn glamorous in a flash. You also should play up your great legs and cheekbones. Your colors are brown, black and white and deep reds.

Aquarius—One-of-a-Kind Looks

Aquarians are unique—like Nastassia Kinski, Cybill Shepherd, Morgan Fairchild. They usually have one especially memorable feature—find it and experiment to show it off to best advantage. Don't be afraid to take risks, try dramatic, interesting effects, like Kim Novak's lavender hair, or Zsa Zsa Gabor's constant dazzle of diamonds. Make your unusual looks work for you; create a memorable image. Prints, plaids and unusual color combinations that no one else can wear work on you. You are one of the few who can carry off the bright psychedelic colors. Be careful not to overdo, however. You can look interesting and provocative, even without shock tactics.

Pisces—The Fantasist

You are the master of illusion and often evoke another, more romantic time and place with your appearance. Like Gloria Vanderbilt, you look wonderful in soft dreamy costume-y clothes that capture the imagination. Play up your beautiful eyes, like Liza Minelli and Liz Taylor. You can portray many moods, so your wardrobe should have a variety of looks from the tweeds of the English countryside, to antibellum laces, to exotica from faraway places. Iridescent fabrics, mermaid sequins, drifty chiffons, and nautical themes are other Pisces possibilities. Since Pisces rules the feet, it follows that beautiful and comfortable shoes are very important. You are very sensitive to chemicals; so test your cosmetics for possible allergies and be sure to protect your delicate skin from the sun. Sea green and violet are your sun sign colors.

15

Scorpio Astro-Outlook for 1988

Your love of mystery and intrigue should be more than satisfied this year, Scorpio. You'll delve into new areas of the occult and could make some startling discoveries—especially about yourself. You'll need more time away from your usual round of events and duties, however. Don't try to carry too heavy a workload.

Since much of your recent financial pressure eases in mid-February, you'll be less money-minded and more concerned with ideas, self-expression and learning. The grand exit of both Saturn and Uranus from your solar money house then should help smooth out some eccentricities in your cash flow as well as take your interests elsewhere.

In your career, look for opportunities in films, writing, art, music, real estate and any profession that allows you to use creativity or imagination. You'll work especially well behind the scenes rather than in front of the crowd.

Romantically, you'll be drawn to calm, helpful, sympathetic types who really listen to what you have to say. Someone born under the sign of Pisces or Virgo should fit the bill. You'll be especially anxious to settle a romantic matter during the first eight days of the year when assertive Mars is in your sign. Both January and October are significant months for serious relationships with the opposite sex.

In addition, the planet of good fortune, Jupiter, will be in your solar house of partnerships and marriage most of the year, beginning in early April. You'll benefit from the kindnesses, benevolence and enthusiastic efforts of a partner, associate, agent or consultant. If you are single, you meet someone who is a definite marriage prospect.

Although others will be helpful, many situations will solved best through your own in-depth self-analysis. Meditate, study, research, look within. Surround yourself with music, beauty, flowers, trees and serene environments. Learn to be alone without feeling lonely. Around September, such activities are especially favored and can result in inspirations that will serve you well in the following year.

For more details, consult your daily guides in the pages ahead.

16

Fifteen Months
of Day-by-Day Predictions

OCTOBER 1987

Thursday, October 1 (Moon in Capricorn to Aquarius 8:51 a.m.)   You receive a favorable response to a recent inquiry regarding business, property, or emotional commitment. Your past efforts win rewards—be ready to confer with an authority figure who has answers you need. Capricorn and Cancer people are on your side today.

Friday, October 2 (Moon in Aquarius)   You'll complete an important project today. Family members are on your side and property matter will be settled harmoniously. Let go of old hurts, wounds, and resentments and look to a brighter future. Aries and Libra people play key roles. Your lucky number is 9.

Saturday, October 3 (Moon in Aquarius to Pisces 10:39 p.m.)   You shake off the old and begin building for the future. You'll have greater freedom, independence, and renewed vitality. Grab an opportunity to get in on "ground floor" of a new venture. Someone with romantic ideas wants to meet you.

Sunday, October 4 (Moon in Pisces)   Avoid abrupt decisions where an affair of the heart is concerned. You'll need time, patience, and a calmer emotional outlook to iron this out. An older woman or loyal family member is on hand, will feed and reassure you, helping to rebuild your confidence. Your lucky number is 2.

Monday, October 5 (Moon in Pisces)   Your optimism surges upward, creativity is high, and you're in the mood for an intriguing adventure. An intellectual member of the opposite sex finds your mind delightful and wants to wine and dine you and spur you on. Some exciting entertainment is in store for you later today.

Tuesday, October 6 (Moon in Pisces to Aries 12:35 a.m.—Eclipse at 11:12 p.m.)   Work, humdrum details, and a challenging obstacle to be overcome occupy you today. You'll win through keeping a steady pace, a determined effort, and your ability to follow rules and regulations. Your co-workers can be transformed into enthusiastic supporters; just stick to the job!

Wednesday, October 7 (Full Moon in Aries)   Changes occur in rapid succession at work. You welcome variety, but are challenged by the full moon excitement in the air. Your best route is to talk it out with one who is restless and impatient. Later, say yes to an unexpected date with your romantic partner.

Thursday, October 8 (Moon in Aries to Taurus 3:57 a.m.)   Marital status, partnerships, and legal affairs are highlighted today. You'll need tact, patience, and a charming manner to untangle the situation. Be willing to listen more than talk; let another make the key decisions. A Libra is involved. Your lucky number is 6.

Friday, October 9 (Moon in Taurus)   See people, places, and relationships as they actually are—foggy thinking could put another on a pedestal which isn't merited. Escapist activities won't help. Be willing to maintain a low profile and play the waiting game. Pisces is in a key role.

Saturday, October 10 (Moon in Taurus to Gemini 10:03 a.m.)   Your business sense picks up; you confer with a partner, then make an enterprising money move. The time is ripe for an intensified relationship, physical gratification, and promises about the future. Capricorn and Cancer share your day. The lucky number is 8.

Sunday, October 11 (Moon in Gemini)   You take stock of your possessions, desires, and ambitions and make a move to clear your life of time-wasting situations. Your financial success depends on seeing the big picture rather than small, petty problems. A sharp, perceptive, aggressive person aids you.

Monday, October 12 (Moon in Gemini to Cancer 7:31 p.m.)   A revived sense of yourself energizes you; you're ready for new beginnings. You dramatize yourself and your deep emotions to one who can grant you love, money, or a fresh start in life. Be ready for a major transformation. Leo and Aquarius people get your attention. Your lucky number is 1.

Tuesday, October 13 (Moon in Cancer)   Focus on in-laws, relatives at a distance, and possible travel plans. You need patience, time and diplomacy to set your long-range plans in motion. Don't give up too soon; play the waiting game. You're in the mood for family, security, and an exercise of your imagination.

Wednesday, October 14 (Moon in Cancer)   Your intellectual curiosity is spurred—you travel, investigate, and probe into opinions and life-styles. A fascinating stranger sees you as a challenge and is intrigued by your humor, optimism, facts, and figures. Don't scatter your forces. Your lucky number is 3.

Thursday, October 15 (Moon in Cancer to Leo 7:34 a.m.) A solid executive type has an eye on you and wants to see if you can deliver under pressure. Stick to the job—don't be tempted to take side trips. A good time can come later; you're building reputation now. Aquarius and Leo are important to you today.

Friday, October 16 (Moon in Leo) Creative thinking and a written document lead to greater prestige and recognition. You'll be magnetic, verbal, and highly attractive to the opposite sex. State your case, let others know what you think. Virgo and Gemini people are interested.

Saturday, October 17 (Moon in Leo to Virgo 8:06 p.m.) A parental figure demands devotion, loyalty, and more of your time. Concentrate on harmonizing a domestic situation. Flowers, a luxury item, and gourmet foods will help set the mood. Display politeness and tact to family members. Your lucky number is 6.

Sunday, October 18 (Moon in Virgo) You work behind the scenes with a group, club, or circle of friends. You feel special, remote from the crowd and can actually play the role of the power behind the throne. Your emotions run deep. You're drawn to humanitarian causes and have compassion for the underdog.

Monday, October 19 (Moon in Virgo) Long-range goals are in the spotlight, including love, marriage, and greater business success. An aura of responsibility surrounds you, leading a prestigious person to offer help. You'll be good at selling, promoting, and organizing. A Capricorn plays a key role.

Tuesday, October 20 (Moon in Virgo to Libra) Erase your fears, doubts, and restricting thoughts—you'll have an opportunity to move beyond your current limitations. A universal viewpoint wins, so does an association with people who are pioneers. Charity work yields results. For luck, play number 9.

Wednesday, October 21 (Moon in Libra)   A secret will be revealed about romance; your creativity will blossom. A dynamic member of the opposite sex is involved in a backstage affair. The key is to throw light on the dark areas and get off to a new start. Leo and Aquarius people intrigue you.

Thursday, October 22 (Moon in Libra to Scorpio 2:42 p.m.)   The new moon accents intuition, feelings, preparation for a new family role. You'll act as a consultant to nurture and aid others and can become too soft over a sad story. Guard against rumors, impressions, and moods. Heal emotional wounds in yourself and others.

Friday, October 23 (Moon in Scorpio)   Your sense of style is accented. You become more aware of your body image and take exciting steps to improve yourself. Travel, learning, and humor are involved in this fast-paced scenario. Be sensible—don't take on more than you can handle. Your lucky number is 3.

Saturday, October 24 (Moon in Scorpio to Sagittarius 7:57 p.m.)   A solid approach is called for in health, diet, and nutrition problems. You become immersed in details, obligations, and possess the will-power to revise and rebuild on a more solid foundation. Aquarius and Leo people are involved. Avoid extremes today!

Sunday, October 25 (Moon in Sagittarius)   A versatile attitude is needed in handling cash, transacting business, or communicating about your romantic desires. You're ready for more freedom, including a brief trip and a chance to make the acquaintance of a brainy person. Your lucky number is 5.

Monday, October 26 (Moon in Sagittarius to Capricorn 11:33 p.m.)   Make a luxury purchase for the home today. With heightened artistic powers you choose the right touches for more harmonious surroundings. Money owed you will be collected and the financial picture will brighten. Libra and Taurus people are in tune with you today.

Tuesday, October 27 (Moon in Capricorn)　You yearn for perfection, beauty, solitude, and want to escape from the local area. Your ideal romance could be all in your mind. Poetry, music, and imagination are favored—write, create, and fantasize. Seek constructive methods of escape. Your lucky number is 7.

Wednesday, October 28 (Moon in Capricorn)　Your drive and ambition are highlighted. You come back to earth, take the lead in a neighborhood project, and make solid promises about the future. A love relationship deepens if you're willing to commit yourself. A prosperous individual seeks out your company.

Thursday, October 29 (Moon in Capricorn to Aquarius 2:27 a.m.)　You'll complete what you started, and envision new, more visionary projects. Evaluate a relationship with a family member; be decisive, not wishy-washy; it's time for fewer restrictions and a more universal viewpoint. Your lucky number is 9.

Friday, October 30 (Moon in Aquarius)　Concentrate on home, family, property, and security. You're willing to take a bold step, start a new adventure, and think about it later. You can influence others in a dramatic manner, including your romantic partner. Create a new pattern you can live with! *HOLD ON TIGHT & GO !*
XX me

Saturday, October 31 (Moon in Aquarius to Pisces 5:19 a.m.)　You slow down, seek relaxation, rest, and the company of younger family members. Expect love and affection, entertainment, and an emotional denouement to a romantic affair. Nostalgia about the past can have a strong effect on the future. your lucky number is 2.

NOVEMBER 1987

Sunday, November 1 (Moon in Pisces) You gain opportunity for greater self-expression, creativity, and a romantic interlude. You'll hurdle obstacles with ease, break free of limitations, and draw a crowd of well-wishers around you. Look for Aries and Libra people.

Monday, November 2 (Moon in Pisces to Aries 8:40 a.m.) A fresh viewpoint about work impresses your daily associates. You'll be bold, assertive, and sure of your own methods. Now you can move ahead, begin new projects, and promote pioneering ideas. A romantic associate is willing to follow your lead. Your lucky number is 1.

Tuesday, November 3 (Moon in Aries) Focus on diet, health, nutrition, and a more peaceful state of mind. Your emotions could rule the day, if you let them. Avoid being critical, impatient, or too wrapped up in your own feelings. A family member proves to be a valuable ally. Show affection!

Wednesday, November 4 (Moon in Aries to Taurus 1:02 p.m.) Your mate, partner, or associate spurs intellectual curiosity. You desire to probe, ask questions, and expand your horizons beyond your humdrum daily activities. Be more selective of your pursuits— let your partner make major decisions. Your lucky number is 3.

Thursday, November 5 (Full Moon in Taurus) Be content with your routine tasks and necessary obligations and concerns. The full moon tugs you in two directions and adds to temptations to go back on your

175

word or escape rules and regulations. Play a low-key role where your partner or the public is involved.

Friday, November 6 (Moon in Taurus to Gemini 7:10 p.m.)   Limitations and restrictions ease, and more travel, talk, and freedom of movement are possible. You encounter a lively, mental type who wants to tell you all. Express yourself with charm and tact—you'll be a winner in a public relations project.

Saturday, November 7 (Moon in Gemini)   Your sense of duty comes surging to the forefront. You'll be asked to help a family member with a budget, loan, or purchase of domestic requirements. Show you care, but draw the line at making another more dependent. Home entertainment is favored; so is number 6.

Sunday, November 8 (Moon in Gemini)   There is a special accent on spiritual values and hidden truths. Your psychic perceptions are acute; you know without being told. You find someone who seems to be on the same mental wavelength, almost a soul-mate. Pisces and Virgo individuals dominate the scene.

Monday, November 9 (Moon in Gemini to Cancer 4:10 p.m.)   Prestige arrives through publishing, travel, or matters at a distance. Your past efforts are ready to pay off. You'll make practical plans for the future, including a more intensified relationship, and ambitious career steps. You may need further training.

Tuesday, November 10 (Moon in Cancer)   You write *finis* to your current project and move to a higher level. A generous, humanitarian philosophy motivates you to seek a cause or group you can help. Break free of petty details; give your mind scope to roam. Aries and Libra people figure in the picture. Number 9 is your best bet.

Wednesday, November 11 (Moon in Cancer to Leo 3:45 p.m.)   Your original ideas are applauded by the higher echelon. You're in line for a new start, promotion, or renewed contract. You dazzle a member of the opposite sex, attract followers, and show the general public your true talents. Your lucky number is 1.

Thursday, November 12 (Moon in Leo)   Nostalgia for the past dominates the scenario. A parent or authority figure wants to talk, reminisce, and share your emotions and feelings. You take time out for tenderness and nurturing. Your family background provides a launching pad for the achievement of security.

Friday, November 13 (Moon in Leo)   A witty, humorous streak in you makes a bid for attention. You display knowledge for all to see in a teaching or learning situation. Energies may be scattered, leading you to diversified ambitious undertakings. Be more selective; choose the right project!

Saturday, November 14 (Moon in Leo to Virgo 4:29 a.m.)   The accent is on hopes, wishes, friendships, and social gatherings. You'll be tempted to go to extremes, but will be a winner through simplifying procedures and taking one step at a time. Be sure your plans are down-to-earth. Your lucky number is 4.

Sunday, November 15 (Moon in Virgo)   Communication is the key to solving problems, working with groups, getting to the heart of matters. You'll be magnetic, wise, romantic, and could become involved with a brainy type. An affair of the heart has a chance to escalate into a grand passion. Go for it!

Monday, November 16 (Moon in Virgo to Libra 3:48 p.m.)   A domestic drama unfolds, with you in the role of peacemaker. Hopes and wishes are tied up with a family gathering, greater harmony, and a possible change of residence. Confidential information will be revealed that helps you tune into the real needs of a loved one.

Tuesday, November 17 (Moon in Libra)   You build a fence around yourself in a bid for peace and quiet, a chance to be alone. You need to discover yourself, trim down to the essentials, and learn the real inside story. Art, music, and intuition are favored. Compassion plays a strong role in the scenario.

Wednesday, November 18 (Moon in Libra to Scorpio 11:47 p.m.)   The accent continues on behind-the-scenes endeavors, but the focus shifts to practical, concrete projects. You win the favor of a key executive, know you are on the way up, and act accordingly. Fears and doubts dissolve in a surge of self-confidence. Your lucky number is 8.

Thursday, November 19 (Moon in Scorpio)   You are in a high lunar cycle, ready to make your influence felt in a wider circle. Petty individuals drop out of the picture, and you meet someone with a worldwide viewpoint, dash, and daring. Express yourself artistically. Write, create, draw, paint, perform!

Friday, November 20 (Moon in Scorpio)   The time is ripe for a new start, including romance, entertainment, and rejuvenation of your personal appearance. The new moon accents physical charisma, intense emotions, and the desire to remake the world and yourself. Dress distinctively. Your lucky number is 1.

Saturday, November 21 (Moon in Scorpio to Sagittarius 4:16 p.m.)   The focus shifts to money, possessions, thoughts of security. Your intuition is riding high, you know instinctively where to spend, where to save. Accept the chance for greater relaxation and attention to family. Allow a romantic matter to develop naturally!

Sunday, November 22 (Moon in Sagittarius)   A light-hearted, good-humored attitude draws friends, popularity, a chance to make money. You're on the move, but your mind is not on details—don't lose things in transit or attempt to handle highly technical matters. Your lucky number is 3.

Monday, November 23 (Moon in Sagittarius to Capricorn 6:32 a.m.)   A favorable moon aspect coincides with the need to catch up, settle down, and write letters or make phone calls. Be satisfied with your routine; excitement is not in your best interest now. Review, revise, and rebuild on a more solid foundation. An Aquarius is in the picture.

Tuesday, November 24 (Moon in Capricorn)   Today brings change, travel, variety, and visits to relatives in your local neighborhood. You're full of ideas, ready to revise plans, and receptive to a last-minute invitation from a fast-talking member of the opposite sex. Your lucky number is 5.

Wednesday, November 25 (Moon in Capricorn to Aquarius 8:13 a.m.)   Your deepest need is for peace, harmony, and better relations with family and loved ones. You'll beautify your surroundings and plan a special get-together, and give gifts. A disruptive influence will be removed in time. Libra, Taurus, and another Scorpio are on the scene.

Thursday, November 26 (Moon in Aquarius)   Spiritual and family values are highlighted. Your sensitivity is increased, but this only makes you better able to relate to the needs of others. You won't feel sorry for yourself if you count your blessings and show compassion to those in need. Your lucky number is 7.

Friday, November 27 (Moon in Aquarius to Pisces 10:40 a.m.)   Now is the time for more practical and ambitious plans. You see a chance to benefit through property, family background, or domestic affairs. An authority figure is on your side and will help to get this new enterprise off the ground. Love and marital status are involved.

Saturday, November 28 (Moon in Pisces)   Your entertainment plans are spotlighted. Your life gains new purpose and greater meaning, as romance blossoms, new friends appear, and you have a chance to display your artistic talents. You'll put an end to indecision as you gain fresh viewpoint. Your lucky number is 9.

Sunday, November 29 (Moon in Pisces to Aries 2:26 p.m.)   You take center stage in performance. Others applaud your charisma, vitality, original ideas. The status quo is out the window. A personal appearance is dramatic and gains the attention of a wide circle of admirers. A Leo is in the picture.

Monday, November 30 (Moon in Aries)   Accept time out with graciousness. The family gathers round, and you wax sentimental, talk about the past and place greater focus on diet, health, and nutrition. An older woman has good advice about work, chores, or other duties. Your lucky number is 2.

DECEMBER 1987

Tuesday, December 1 (Moon in Aries to Taurus 8:06 p.m.)   New approaches are favored in your work and health. You originate, promote, make sales, and blaze trails for others to follow. You'll work with someone you love or admire, finding pleasure in everyday activities together. Number 1 could bring you luck today.

Wednesday, December 2 (Moon in Taurus)   A slower pace and more dependence on the good will of others is indicted. You work with the public, but in a nurturing, caring way—competition is out of the picture. Your intuition proves a strong ally in affair of the heart. Go with your feelings for the best results.

Thursday, December 3 (Moon in Taurus)   Travel, parties, intellectual stimulation brighten your day. You'll be restless to do your own thing but may have to play the waiting game. Let your partner, mate, or associate handle the details of technical matters and legalities. A Sagittarius is on your wave length.

Friday, December 4 (Moon in Taurus to Gemini 3:13 a.m.)   The financial picture depends on a dedicated effort and the ability to follow through on a project rather than chasing rainbows. Straighten out joint monies, and figure out what to spend and what to save. Make lists; pay bills. Your lucky number is 4.

Saturday, December 5 (Full Moon in Gemini)   You fall under the spell of someone intriguing and could undergo a magical transformation. Conflicts exist with the full moon in the skies, but you'll get to the heart of matters through much talk and probing of other's ideas and values.

Sunday, December 6 (Moon in Gemini to Cancer 12:20 p.m.)   Expenses for family pleasures will be covered by a generous person. Be prepared for travel, expansion of your viewpoint, and spiritual revelation. A sense of duty to others surges to the forefront. Taurus and Libra are important to you now.

Monday, December 7 (Moon in Cancer)   A glamorous visitor from afar adds to the excitement of the season. You learn to know yourself better by dealing with foreign ideas, customs, and persons. You'll transcend petty prejudice and understand more about religious history. Your lucky number is 7.

Tuesday, December 8 (Moon in Cancer to Leo 11:40 p.m.)   Money, investments, and import-export activities occupy you today. You'll be in an excellent position to make deals with those in power. Merchandise ordered from a catalog or from an advertisement arrives. Capricorn and Cancer people communicate today.

Wednesday, December 9 (Moon in Leo)   Recognition and career interests are favored. You deal with management level and widen your appeal through pioneering ideas. Rid yourself of petty fears, doubts, and selfish motives—now is time to take charge of your life. Your lucky number is 9.

Thursday, December 10 (Moon in Leo)   You'll have a chance to prove yourself in a "take charge" situation. This is no time to take a back seat—you have too much to offer, including originality, determination, and the backing of a member of opposite sex who finds you romantically attractive.

Friday, December 11 (Moon in Leo to Virgo 12:30 p.m.)   You'll win your way through diplomacy, rather than forcing issues. Rewards from professional accomplishments flow easily when you relax and allow things to take their natural course. Trust a lucky hunch. An older woman you encounter at a gathering has good answers.

Saturday, December 12 (Moon in Virgo)   The pace quickens, invitations appear for parties, meetings, and group activities. You'll be in high good humor, sought after, and ready to pit your wits against an agile-minded member of the opposite sex. Travel could be in your plans. Your lucky number is 3.

Sunday, December 13 (Moon in Virgo)   You make progress with hopes and goals through self-discipline, patience, and the willingness to maintain steady pace. A friend with a solid reputation can be a strong ally, but don't hand over the details to another. Aquarius and Leo persons demand attention.

Monday, December 14 (Moon in Virgo to Libra 12:40 a.m.)   A secret is revealed regarding your romantic life. You'll gain more confidence for the future if you discuss matters with a loved one, get to the heart of problems. Don't allow jealousy or insecurity to disturb you; right answers are available. Your lucky number is 5.

Tuesday, December 15 (Moon in Libra)   Diplomatic family differences can be completely resolved behind the scenes. Seek luxury surroundings, gourmet food, and artistic or musical entertainment. You'll achieve harmony through seeing both sides of the question; be willing to compromise.

Wednesday, December 16 (Moon in Libra to Scorpio 9:41 a.m.)   Psychic and intuitive powers bring the answers you need. An aura of glamour, beauty, and mystery surrounds you, causing others to be reluctant to approach; but they are impresed by your image. Light will be shed on darkness as the day progresses. Your lucky number is 7.

Thursday, December 17 (Moon in Scorpio)   The lunar cycle is high; you're in the driver's seat and will impress others with your stamina, achievements, and the backing of prestigious persons. A love affair intensifies, marital status is discussed, and you make long-term commitments. A Capricorn is in the spotlight.

Friday, December 18 (Moon in Scorpio to Sagittarius 2:33 p.m.)   Your magnetic personal appeal makes this a "banner day" if you rise above your petty interests. You'll deal best with big projects, humanitarian endeavors, and people who have one foot in the future. Your life is about to take a fascinating new turn.

Saturday, December 19 (Moon in Sagittarius)   You'll profit through original methods and inventive ideas. A dramatic Leo type wants to wine and dine you with romance in mind. Be willing to spend money on your appearance, including distinctive new accessories. Your lucky number is 1.

Sunday, December 20 (Moon in Sagittarius to Capricorn 4:08 p.m.)   The new moon places greater accent on security, savings, and ways to help family members. Avoid abrupt decisions or forcing the issue. You'll need time out to figure plans and listen to the wisdom of your own intuition. Cancer and Capricorn people are involved.

Monday, December 21 (Moon in Capricorn)   Today brings close kin, neighbors, and an active social life in your local area. A message or individual from afar arrives on the scene, adding to confusion as well as joy. Maintain a light touch, a sense of humor, and the ability to be open to the plans of others.

Tuesday, December 22 (Moon in Capricorn to Aquarius 4:20 p.m.)   You make order out of chaos, catching up with a mountain of details, and overcoming what seem to be insurmountable obstacles. Discard frills and stick to practical methods that work. Time is limited; don't digress from your main goal. For luck, try number 4.

Wednesday, December 23 (Moon in Aquarius)   An intellectual pal arrives at your base of operations, bringing a breath of fresh air. You change plans at a moment's notice, make brief trips, and are surprisingly open to a romantic invitation. Communication is the key to enjoyment in family relationships.

Thursday, December 24 (Moon in Aquarius to Pisces 5:10 p.m.)   A family get-together is on the agenda, with you in role of decorator, peace-maker, and diplomat. Your home will be beautified and a disturbing element removed. A luxury gift puts all in a better mood, so does music and entertainment. Your lucky number is 6.

Friday, December 25 (Moon in Pisces)   An aura of mystery and romance surrounds pleasures today. You'll

184

be inspired to help those less fortunate, including special visits to entertain persons confined to home or hospital. You are very interested in psychic experiences today. So is a Pisces friend.

Saturday, December 26 (Moon in Pisces to Aries 8:05 p.m.) Love, marital status, and greater commitments about the future are spotlighted. You'll have a chance to attend a prestigious theater production or meet persons involved with entertainment and recreation. Your standing in the community is enhanced. Your lucky number is 8.

Sunday, December 27 (Moon in Aries) A humanitarian and charitable endeavor gives you the chance to widen your personal appeal through service to others. You come up with a big, new idea, and are able to promote it on a grand scale. The medical and employment problems of others concern you and keep you busy.

Monday, December 28 (Moon in Aries) Don't expect the status quo—new contacts give you access to job information that helps you make a fresh start. You invent and promote original ideas and express love for another through deeds rather than words. Leo and Aquarius persons are in your life now.

Tuesday, December 29 (Moon in Aries to Taurus 1:37 a.m.) A cooperative role is best today. You'll be able to catch up after a period of frenzied activity and will be more interested in domestic concerns than outside activities. Play a waiting game where decisions are needed or let your partner make them. Your lucky number is 2.

Wednesday, December 30 (Moon in Taurus) You deal with the general public in a bright, active manner. This can include travel, teaching, sales, or a witty mental exchanges. You'll have the tendency to take on more than you can handle. Sagittarius and Gemini individuals figure prominently.

Thursday, December 31 (Moon in Taurus to Gemini 9:29 a.m.) You'll play a practical, hard-working role in celebrations—and may feel expenses are getting out of hand. Keep your eye on the details, read between the lines, and follow through on what you have promised, but without unnecessary frills. Your lucky number is 4.

JANUARY 1988

Friday, January 1 (Moon in Gemini) Resolve to forget the past and turn over a new leaf. This pertains particularly to possessions and passions shared with another person. You'll fare better if you look at the big picture and dismiss petty grudges. Your lucky number is 9.

Saturday, January 2 (Moon in Gemini to Cancer 7:15 p.m.) You'll make a new start in a new direction. Creativity and romance could be part of the picture; it all depends on your willingness to assume a more generous, openhearted attitude towards a close associate. Travel is favored later in the day.

Sunday, January 3 (Moon in Cancer) Old memories of long-ago and far-away come streaming back into your consciousness. You may want to take a sentimental journey to visit distant relatives or old neighborhoods. An individual who "remembers you when" wants to know what you're doing now.

Monday, January 4 (Moon in Cancer) Your curiosity about the world is stimulated. You'll want to know, to learn, to investigate, and find out how other people

186

live. Someone who has traveled widely has tales to tell you—you'll be drawn into a fascinating social situation. Have fun!

Tuesday, January 5 (Moon in Cancer to Leo 6:47 a.m.) You'll gain recognition for your resourcefulness. Pitch in and do the jobs that have to be done. This will include dealing with many details, cutting through red tape, and impressing a superior with your diligence and talents. Your lucky number is 4.

Wednesday, January 6 (Moon in Leo) A "way with words" could win a promotion or a brand-new image in your career. Be open to stimulating new ideas that are circulating. There's enough going on around you to keep you busy and excited. A romantic invitation seems likely from a Gemini type.

Thursday, January 7 (Moon in Leo to Virgo 7:35 p.m.) The accent is on loyalty, devotion, and sentiment. Others will turn to you for leadership, friendship and help with their problems. You'll feel very responsible for others—don't overdo this and take on burdens not rightly yours. Libra plays a role.

Friday, January 8 (Moon in Virgo) Look within for the answers to hopes and dreams. No group or organization can give you what you need right now. Accent spiritual tendencies; get to know yourself better. Some time spent alone in personal research is your best bet. Your lucky number is 7.

Saturday, January 9 (Moon in Virgo) This is a power-play day. Take full advantage of every opportunity to advance your position. Authority figures will help. Romantic promises or commitments can be made that will be fulfilling and lasting. Capricorn and Cancer are on the scene.

Sunday, January 10 (Moon in Virgo to Libra 8:17 a.m.)   Look behind the scenes for answers. A new level of awareness enables you to bring a large-scale project to completion. You'll be a supersleuth in ferreting out secrets if you adopt a loving, humanitarian attitude. Help someone without telling a soul.

Monday, January 11 (Moon in Libra)   Your quest for originality, romance, and a livelier social life may be repressed by current circumstances. You'll have some important projects to unveil very soon, but don't jump the gun. Artistic expression is your best outlet now. Count on number 1.

Tuesday, January 12 (Moon in Libra to Scorpio 6:39 p.m.)   You'll stride easily into a high lunar cycle, practically unnoticed, but winning your way, nevertheless. Intuitively, you know just where you're headed, but may not be able to tell the reason why. Emotionally, you'll be drawn to gentle, home-loving types.

Wednesday, January 13 (Moon in Scorpio)   Social activities and opportunities abound. Put your best foot forward; your sense of grooming and style is at a high point. Others will view you as light, bright, humorous and witty, but may not take your ideas very seriously; so just have fun. The lucky number is 3.

Thursday, January 14 (Moon in Scorpio to Sagittarius 12:58 a.m.)   Practical, personal details must be dealt with. You'll have the discipline to carry through on diet, exercise, and other regimes to improve your health. Follow the rules; take matters one step at a time. Aquarius and Leo figure prominently.

Friday, January 15 (Moon in Sagittarius)   Today's emphasis is on ideas, books, manuscripts and special knowledge you have recently gained. You'll see ways to make your education and training pay off handsomely.

Promote yourself and your talents; you'll be inspired by someone of the opposite sex who believes in you.

Saturday, January 16 (Moon in Sagittarius to Capricorn 3:15 a.m.)   Take advantage of sales or gift money to purchase luxury items for the home. Your taste for beauty, style, texture and design will be enhanced. Someone you love will appreciate what you buy, create or envision now. Family life shows definite improvement.

Sunday, January 17 (Moon in Sagittarius to Capricorn 3:15 a.m.)   Ideas are likely to be highly imaginative, but impractical. You'll be strongly motivated to escape the everyday routine in favor of flights of fancy. Don't allow ultra-sensitivity to the words or opinions of others to hurt your feelings. Pisces is in the picture.

Monday, January 18 (Moon in Capricorn)   Follow through on promises. You'll gain prestige in local area through leadership abilities. Others will see you as strong and dependable, an authority in some special field. A romantic commitment may be asked for or given. The lucky number is 8.

Tuesday, January 19 (Moon in Capricorn to Aquarius 3:02 a.m.)   A project concerning home or real estate will be completed. Now is the time to re-evaluate where you stand and make large-scale plans for the future. Be generous with a family member who comes to you for help, but don't create over-dependence. An Aries is involved.

Wednesday, January 20 (Moon in Aquarius)   The stage is set at home base for a dramatic scenario. You'll impress close associates with your generosity and charisma. New start in new direction is favored in your home life. Someone with great need for applause wants to win your heart. For luck, try number 1.

Thursday, January 21 (Moon in Aquarius to Pisces 2:27 a.m.)   The emphasis is on creativity, entertainment and romance. An easygoing, emotional individual is involved. Don't be afraid to reveal your deeper feelings to this person—you'll be understood and appreciated. Cooperation you require will be granted.

Friday, January 22 (Moon in Pisces)   An entertaining day is on the agenda. You'll go places, do things and capture more than one heart. Invitations will be plentiful—be discriminating in selection of parties, dinners, or other social events. Sagittarius and Gemini play key roles.

Saturday, January 23 (Moon in Pisces to Aries 3:31 a.m.)   Service to others is emphasized. Stick to chores that are rightfully yours; don't attempt to escape or evade rules and regulations. A momentous amount of work can be accomplished by taking one step at a time and sticking to a schedule. The lucky number is 4.

Sunday, January 24 (Moon in Aries)   You'll feel more free to express yourself in creative, original ways. New methods of accomplishing old chores can be used to your advantage. Small animals, dependents and others in your care can charm you with their humorous ways. Gemini and Virgo are in the picture.

Monday, January 25 (Moon in Aries to Taurus 7:36 a.m.)   Play the waiting game; don't force issues now. You can accomplish much through weighing and balancing matters, catering to the whims and desires of a partner, mate or associate. Special emphasis is on marital status. Libra and Taurus are concerned.

Tuesday, January 26 (Moon in Taurus)   The search for an ideal is featured. Don't be disillusioned if an associate turns out to be less perfect than you imagined. You'll fare best through selfless service to others—feeling sorry for yourself is not recommended. A Pisces could be your best confidante.

Wednesday, January 27 (Moon in Taurus to Gemini 3:02 p.m.)   Consult someone who has the learning or experience you lack. Information gained will enable you to make wise moves at the correct times. Honor, prestige and money come to you through association with one in the limelight. Your lucky number is 8.

Thursday, January 28 (Moon in Gemini)   Financial affairs demand big thinking, bold steps, and a pioneering attitude. Someone with a strong competitive streak can tell you where to get the best values for your money. Be generous with those less fortunate than yourself. An Aries is in the picture.

Friday, January 29 (Moon in Gemini)   Romance sizzles, and your emotional involvement deepens. You'll receive the admiration of one who loves drama, sports and adventure. This could be the start of something big! Wear bright colors, be willing to capture the limelight. Your lucky number is 1.

Saturday, January 30 (Moon in Gemini to Cancer 1:11 a.m.)   One who taught you in the past returns. There's much to discuss, including travel and educational plans. You'll take much on faith, without having to be given logical reasons for everything. Family members contribute to expansive feelings. Go places together.

Sunday, January 31 (Moon in Cancer)   A stranger with intriguing ideas dominates the picture. You'll be restless to explore beyond your current boundaries. Enjoy foreign foods, cultures and personalities. Popularity and social life are on a meteoric rise. A Sagittarian convinces you to take a chance!

FEBRUARY 1988

Monday, February 1 (Moon in Cancer to Leo 1:06 p.m.)   Promote your career and capture new fields.

You'll be able to advance your personal interests among people of influence. You'll charm someone in authority, possibly born under the sign of Leo. Be ready for romance, special entertainment and a new direction.

Tuesday, February 2 (Moon in Leo)   Life slows down somewhat, giving you a chance to save time, money and energy. A cooperative venture brings you in touch with a sensitive, shy person, who treats you as one of the family. A special knack for making money and using it wisely puts you far ahead.

Wednesday, February 3 (Moon in Leo)   You'll break out of an emotional rut. New mental interests keep you busy; you'll want to travel far to investigate a particular idea. Results put you in the public eye, making new friends and teaching others what you know. A Sagittarius plays a key role.

Thursday, February 4 (Moon in Leo to Virgo 1:54 a.m.)   You'll get what you want, but will have to work hard to earn it. Don't take anything for granted; be willing to review, revise and rebuild on a new basis, if necessary. Resist the impulse to let chores slide while you socialize. Your lucky number is 4.

Friday, February 5 (Moon in Virgo)   A romantic wish comes true. You'll meet someone who suits you mentally, physically and emotionally. Be yourself; show who you really are—you'll gain love and admiration from one who is looking for someone just like you. A heart-to-heart talk reveals all.

Saturday, February 6 (Moon in Virgo to Libra 2:36 p.m.)   Conditions improve at home, especially if you take the responsibility for straightening out family differences. You'll desire luxury in surroundings, gourmet food and quiet entertainment in your own abode. Libra is in the picture. So is number 6.

Sunday, February 7 (Moon in Libra)   You'll be highly subjective, sensitive and attuned to mysteries, secrets and psychic experiences. Confront your own fears and doubts, then deal with them realistically. Spiritual values will sustain you; don't be too materialistic. You'll find yourself!

Monday, February 8 (Moon in Libra)   An object of your affection proves love and loyalty. You'll fare best as the power behind the scenes, pulling strings and preparing for an enterprising new step. Get advice from one who could be called "the voice of experience." And try number 8.

Tuesday, February 9 (Moon in Libra to Scorpio 1:42 a.m.)   Your personal plans require a note of daring. Let go of foolish fears and take a strong new stand. You'll be out in the open, projecting your true personality. Wear bold colors, associate with dynamic types. You can vastly increase your sphere of influence in the world.

Wednesday, February 10 (Moon in Scorpio)   The high lunar cycle and desire for a fresh new start will take you anywhere you want to go. Romance, entertainment and self-expression play prominent roles. You'll be in the right place at the right time if you listen to intuitive good sense. Your lucky number is 1.

Thursday, February 11 (Moon in Scorpio to Sagittarius 9:36 a.m.)   You'll collect money due you and the urge to save will help you hang onto it. Forego extravagances in favor of security, home and family interests. This is not the time to begin new projects or make forceful moves. A loved one, possibly a Cancer, will understand.

Friday, February 12 (Moon in Sagittarius)   The restless pursuit of intellectual values could take you far afield from your original destination. You're in the mood to overdo, but others will be lenient with you. Your bright, happy mood could be the reason others are drawn to you. Your lucky number is 3.

Saturday, February 13 (Moon in Sagittarius to Capricorn 1:36 p.m.)   Now is the time to attend to details. No one else is going to handle personal interests as well as you. This includes keeping track of expenses and catching up with correspondence. Shopping for practical items could also be on your busy agenda.

Sunday, February 14 (Moon in Capricorn)   You'll break free from routine as the emphasis shifts to variety, exchange of ideas, and an exciting journey. A member of the opposite sex wants to compare interests and see if they blend. A relative turns up at your door unexpectedly. The lucky number is 5.

Monday, February 15 (Moon in Capricorn to Aquarius 2:25 p.m.)   You'll be the "master diplomat" in a discussion with a loved one. Settle all disagreements peaceably, but don't allow others to walk all over you. This applies especially to a dominant family member who needs attention, affection. A Taurus is in the picture.

Tuesday, February 16 (Moon in Aquarius)   The urge to walk alone should be honored, especially if you need time out to reassess your feelings and desires. You may be concerned about real estate values, profits, and unique ideas about your life-style. Your Scorpio ability to keep a secret will be accented.

Wednesday, February 17 (Moon in Aquarius to Pisces 1:44 p.m.)   Long-range romantic prospects are emphasized. You won't be interested in light flirtations or frivolous entertainment. Someone with a strong sense of responsibility wins your heart. Ask the question you've had on your mind for so long. And try number 8, today.

Thursday, February 18 (Moon in Pisces)   Your appreciation for the arts is enhanced. Music, writing and literature are favored. Attendance at cultural affair will bring you in contact with someone who helps you break away from limitations of the past, perhaps an Aries or Libra.

Friday, February 19 (Moon in Pisces to Aries 1:35 p.m.)   Your creative juices flow, love is favored, and new forms of expression are on the agenda. What started out as a fun project could turn out to be a source of profitable work. Promote original ideas. A Leo will be a real inspiration. Your lucky number is 1.

Saturday, February 20 (Moon in Aries)   Be willing to take a back seat and let others do the driving. The need to nurture others is evident. You'll enjoy food, cooking and light domestic chores. Maintain a low-key attitude—don't give way to fleeting emotions or moods. Be more aware of diet.

Sunday, February 21 (Moon in Aries to Taurus 3:50 p.m.)   Cooperative ventures succeed. You'll attract greater generosity and can benefit through meeting the public. Be ready with answers to questions you'll probably be asked. You'll take special delight in sharing information. A Sagittarian figures prominently.

Monday, February 22 (Moon in Taurus)   You'll gain great satisfaction from a job well done. Emphasize the practical, discard frills, make sure you follow rules and regulations. A partner, mate or associate is watching you, testing your ability to follow through capably. Your lucky number is 4.

Tuesday, February 23 (Moon in Taurus to Gemini 9:42 p.m.)   A love affair gains greater depth. Learn the inside story in order to truly understand the object of your affection. A versatile attitude, readiness to change directions at a moment's notice may be needed. The relationship could be completely transformed.

Wednesday, February 24 (Moon in Gemini) A sentimental gift makes the difference between family harmony and discord. Show that you care, cook a special meal or take a loved one out to a sumptuous dinner. Money matters will improve if you share resources. Libra and Taurus figure prominently.

Thursday, February 25 (Moon in Gemini) Think twice about a financial offer. You won't get "something for nothing" in this instance. Accent occult and spiritual values instead of concentrating on material gain. Someone of a highly compassionate nature is ready to listen. The lucky number is 7.

Friday, February 26 (Moon in Cancer 7:12 a.m.) Business plans succeed beyond your expectations. Be willing to go far afield to impress a superior. This includes dealing with foreign countries, travel, and additional job training. Avoid any kind of limited viewpoint. Capricorn plays a key role.

Saturday, February 27 (Moon in Cancer) A cultural event helps you to realize personal goals. Special emphasis is. on art, music, drama and literature. Set aside more mundane duties in order to stretch your mind. You'll meet a fascinating Aries who wants to play the role of personal mentor.

Sunday, February 28 (Moon in Cancer to Leo 7:12 p.m.) A romantic adventure is on the agenda. Throw off dependence upon others and accent self-reliance. Someone from an entirely different background appears and enlightens you. Be daring and original—someone of the opposite sex will love you for it. Your lucky number is 1.

Monday, February 29 (Moon in Leo)   Be willing to take a secondary role. Someone with great wisdom and extensive experience has much to tell you, but requires your cooperation. You'll gain through conservative, well-thought-out plans. Impatience or worry could only slow you down now.

MARCH 1988

Tuesday, March 1 (Moon in Leo)   You'll be caught up in duties and obligations to family members. Go along in a cooperative effort; pool resources, if necessary, to obtain objectives. Your intuition and sense of timing will be right on target. You'll dine in high style.

Wednesday, March 2 (Moon in Leo to Virgo 8:06 a.m.)   A long-distance call gives you the go-ahead you need. Your hopes and dreams will soon be fulfilled. Former errors will be overlooked, but others may not take you as seriously as you would like. Maintain your sense of humor. Your lucky number is 3.

Thursday, March 3 (Moon in Virgo)   You'll gain satisfaction from a job well done. It may be necessary to cut back on social activities you've planned in order to complete a vital project. Don't be annoyed; proceed in a planned, orderly manner. An Aquarius plays a key role.

Friday, March 4 (Moon in Virgo to Libra 8:32 p.m.) Be prepared for change, travel, variety and a secret meeting regarding romantic feelings. You'll learn what you wanted to know, but may be disappointed if you hold rigidly to old ways of thinking. Gemini and Virgo figure prominently.

Saturday, March 5 (Moon in Libra)   Love of luxury, beauty and art is featured. Don't be disappointed if wishes are not gratified immediately; you may have to settle a family disagreement first. Display love rather than pettiness, especially for one who comes to you with a problem.

Sunday, March 6 (Moon in Libra)   You'll find answers behind the scenes. Spiritual needs must be met before you can face the busy world. Feeling sorry for yourself will only delay your rewards. You'll receive inspirational thoughts from a Pisces with a big heart. The lucky number is 7.

Monday, March 7 (Moon in Libra to Scorpio 7:27 a.m.)   You can step forward with confidence now. Love, money and prestige are on the agenda. The high lunar cycle assures you the respect and leadership opportunities you desire. Strike while the iron is hot in a super power play. A Capricorn is in the picture.

Tuesday, March 8 (Moon in Scorpio)   Your sphere of influence widens. Now is the time to let go of old personal habits that stand in the way of advancement. Artistic, humanitarian, and pioneering goals are within reach. Seek the cooperation of an Aries. Your lucky number is 9.

Wednesday, March 9 (Moon in Scorpio to Sagittarius 3:59 p.m.)   A dynamic person will have a business proposition for you. This will give you the chance to display originality and flair for drama. Romance is also in the picture if you desire; you'll be wined and dined in style. Wear bright colors!

Thursday, March 10 (Moon in Sagittarius)   You'll win your way by diplomacy rather than force. The money you need will be forthcoming; be patient. You need time now to sort out values and investigate profitable new schemes. Let your excellent intuition guide you. And trust number 2.

Friday, March 11 (Moon in Sagittarius to Capricorn)
Don't be confused by a financial offer made today. A discussion could be merely whimsical rather than based on solid fact. You'll meet an unusual person from out of town with an excellent sense of humor. Laugh and accept the chance to be entertained.

Saturday, March 12 (Moon in Capricorn) A serious effort to catch up with paperwork and correspondence will succeed. Keep plugging away. You may feel restricted by a lack of fun and games, but can overcome great obstacles in practical endeavors. An Aquarius figures prominently.

Sunday, March 13 (Moon in Capricorn) Restrictions lift and an opportunity for travel is at hand. Explore your local area for fascinating new places and people. Romantic opportunities are more plentiful than you expect—open lines of communication. You'll be lucky with number 5.

Monday, March 14 (Moon in Capricorn to Aquarius 12:08 a.m.) Home, family, real estate and domestic matters hold the potential for much gain. A change of residence or alteration in current living quarters needs to be dealt with. Beautification of your property would certainly be to your advantage. Ask Libra how.

Tuesday, March 15 (Moon in Aquarius) The accent is on secrets, privacy and hidden factors that need to be analyzed. Take care to avoid self-deception where those you love are concerned. You may be suffering unnecessarily because of a false impression. A Pisces has good advice.

Wednesday, March 16 (Moon in Aquarius to Pisces 12:42 a.m.) A love affair deepens, leading to promises and commitments. You're willing to take the long-range view where marriage and extra responsibilities

199

are involved. The valued opinion of an older person will help you make up mind. Your lucky number is 8.

Thursday, March 17 (Moon in Pisces)   Entertainment plans take you far afield of your original destination. If you assume a universal viewpoint, you'll reach many people with a message of good cheer. Be willing to cut off a relationship with one who has limited you unecessarily.

Friday, March 18 (Moon in Pisces to Aries 12:45 a.m.)   The bright light of attention shines on you in performing your regular duties. You'll accomplish more because you've seen original ways of improving job. A romantic aura surrounds you; a member of opposite sex will pursue you. Your lucky number is 1.

Saturday, March 19 (Moon in Aries)   The focus falls on diet and health. You can improve your appearance by watching your weight and giving yourself more time to relax. Enjoy quiet time with family members, especially someone who has recently appeared from out of your past for a reunion.

Sunday, March 20 (Moon in Aries to Taurus 2:05 a.m.)   Be flexible to plans of partner, mate or associate. You'll be popular, sought after and admired—but would do better to let other persons make the first move socially. Participation in a social affair keeps you on the go. Your lucky number is 3.

Monday, March 21 (Moon in Taurus)   Listen to the proposition of a solid citizen with solid ideas. You'll gain through letting another take the lead. Be satisfied with handling minor details, organizing records and restoring faith of others in you. Don't allow an Aquarian to distract you.

Tuesday, March 22 (Moon in Taurus to Gemini 6:21 a.m.)   You'll intrigue a partner with creative thinking. Your ability to tell a story and capture romantic imagination is accented. A strong magnetic attraction leads to a delightful encounter and places the relationship on an entirely new basis. Your lucky number is 5.

Wednesday, March 23 (Moon in Gemini)   A joint financial effort will bring greater success, love and harmony into your life. Accept gifts that are offered; you can be generous in return with loyalty and devotion. Luxury purchase for the home adds to your pleasures. Libra plays a role.

Thursday, March 24 (Moon in Gemini to Cancer 2:27 p.m.)   An air of mystery surrounds you. You'll want to delve into secrets, especially about love, life, death and afterlife. Take advantage of a travel opportunity, especially if it gets you away to an inspiring retreat from the everyday world. Your best bet is number 7.

Friday, March 25 (Moon in Cancer)   Your mind will be on the future, especially taking profitable steps to improve your knowledge and abilities. Contact with foreign shores adds to your profits; you'll know how to wind up a deal that can make big money. A Capricorn figures in the picture.

Saturday, March 26 (Moon in Cancer)   The emphasis is on spreading the word, advertising, promotion and publishing. Concentrate on the big picture; petty persons who want to restrict your wide interests should be avoided. Grand humanitarian gesture will succeed. Your lucky number is 9.

Sunday, March 27 (Moon in Cancer to Leo 1:54 a.m.)   A new start in a new direction takes you to the top. You'll mix with prestigious people and can ask favors with great success. You'll be a trend-setter, not a follower today—be proud of the recognition you receive. Leo shows admiration.

Monday, March 28 (Moon in Leo)　　You've started things in motion; now don't be impatient for immediate results. Cooperate with one in power who knows you well and values your support. The money situation is bound to improve and security needs will be satisfied. Your lucky number is 2.

Tuesday, March 29 (Moon in Leo to Virgo 2:49 p.m.)　　Your lighthearted mood will attract good business opportunities and unusual individuals who want to share social times. You may have more invitations than you can handle. Be discriminating—choose the best. A Sagittarian is in the picture.

Wednesday, March 30 (Moon in Virgo)　　Don't excpect excitement; be content with the satisfaction that comes from following through on assignments. You may feel closed in, but it won't last long. You can handle special details for friends, groups or organizations. The lucky number is 4.

Thursday, March 31 (Moon in Virgo)　　Romantic dreams promise much; it will be up to you to be where the action is. Break away from a rigid schedule and be open to last-minute invitations. Hearts that are in tune will meet through common interests. Gemini and Virgo are involved.

APRIL 1988

Friday, April 1 (Moon in Virgo to Libra 3:05 a.m.) Investigate behind the scenes. Your natural curiosity will turn up some curious facts. Research, teaching and expansion of mental interests will keep you busy. A cheerful attitude can overcome any feeling of limitation. Your lucky number is 3.

Saturday, April 2 (Moon in Libra)　　Finish what you have started, paying special attention to rules and regulations. Work done behind the scenes continues to be your best bet. You'll get the glory later; now you require privacy and protection from interruptions. Demand it.

Sunday, April 3 (Moon in Libra to Scorpio 1:26 p.m.)   A more creative, romantic, social time begins, especially as the day progresses and you come out of your shell. You'll be sick of restrictions, ready to tell all and to experience new feelings and sensations. You can make the first move romantically.

Monday, April 4 (Moon in Scorpio)   Self-expression in artistic, literary ways is favored. You'll be concerned with colors, designs and fabrics and could use these aptitudes to improve both your own appearance and your surroundings. Stubborn Taurus can be placated through charm.

Tuesday, April 5 (Moon in Scorpio to Sagittarius 9:29 p.m.)   Gain comes from working behind the scenes. You'll emerge as a mysterious, glamorous source of influence. Someone who is attracted will promise you the moon, but may not be very stable. Verify facts; get details in writing.

Wednesday, April 6 (Moon in Sagittarius)   This is a better financial day. Your feet will be on the ground, and an executive will realize this. Ask for a raise or promotion that is due you. You'll get what you deserve, including the backing of a more experienced person. Your lucky number is 8.

Thursday, April 7 (Moon in Sagittarius)   Now is the time to take stock of possessions. Weed out items that you no longer use; repair or revise what can be reclaimed. Cut losses where substantial investments are concerned. Stick with products with a real future. An Aries person can advise you.

Friday, April 8 (Moon in Sagittarius to Capricorn 3:19 a.m.)   Renewed vitality spurs you into greater activity. Your local area becomes the scene of wheeling and dealing with those who share your daily pursuits. You'll express yourself dramatically in speaking and writing, causing a Leo to take special notice.

Saturday, April 9 (Moon in Capricorn)   Intimate conversation with a loved one reveals emotional facts you have been waiting to hear. Don't force issues, however. A patient, uncritical manner can help another to open up about current problems and conflicts. Good food plays a key role.

Sunday, April 10 (Moon in Capricorn to Aquarius 7:10 a.m.)   Tackle one thing at a time around the home. You'll have a long list of things to do that could leave you breathless. You'll probably be constantly diverted by phone calls or people dropping by. Sagittarius and Gemini figure prominently.

Monday, April 11 (Moon in Aquarius)   The spotlight falls on practical matters. Discard frills and empty promises and apply genuine effort to improving the home situation. You'll realize the need for settling down and taking life more seriously. Keep to your schedule. Your lucky number is 4.

Tuesday, April 12 (Moon in Aquarius to Pisces 9:24 a.m.)   Be open to romantic overtures. A period of rapid change and variety is on the agenda when anything can be expected. This applies especially to entertainment, recreation and love affairs. You'll attract mental, analytical types who write, teach or lecture.

Wednesday, April 13 (Moon in Pisces)   The accent is on a sentimental get-together. You may have much to do with making arrangements for the entertainment, food or decorations. You'll feel responsible for showing others a good time, even if it means acting as peace-maker in a quarrel.

Thursday, April 14 (Moon in Pisces to Aries 10:47 a.m.) You'll be wise to retreat and withdraw from an active role. You may still want to help others, especially those who elicit your heightened sympathies, but don't go too far. You need time to get to know yourself better. Look inward. And stick with number 7.

Friday, April 15 (Moon in Aries) A leadership role is expected of you in daily endeavors. You'll find yourself automatically taking over in some small crisis, even if it means losing out on fun. You'll gain in prestige and reputation. Someone at the top is watching to see how you do.

Saturday, April 16 (Moon in Aries to Taurus 12:31 p.m.) An old burden will be lifted, possibly a long-lasting health problem. You'll gain new insight into the probable cause behind your symptoms. Consult a forward-looking person on methods to continue your progress. Release old worries and watch improvement.

Sunday, April 17 (Moon in Taurus) You'll be intrigued by adventure, romance, and a new start in a cooperative venture. You can contribute original ideas without having to take over the project. Your marital status is also in the spotlight; you'll have thoughts about revising goals and desires.

Monday, April 18 (Moon in Taurus to Gemini 4:10 p.m.) The accent is on security, catching up with bill-paying and winning your way through diplomacy rather than force. A partner, mate or associate wants your complete attention and devotion. You'll play the role of indulgent parent, if wise. Your lucky number is 2.

Tuesday, April 19 (Moon in Gemini) A generous gift will be received, putting you in a lighter, brighter mood. An important contact can be made at a party, gathering or conference. Dig deep for the answers, satisfy curiosity regarding the mysteries of life. A Sagittarian figures in the picture.

Wednesday, April 20 (Moon in Gemini to Cancer 11:04 p.m.)   Practical aspects of the financial picture are accented. Obtain wise advice on taxes, insurance and bank accounts. Take the necessary steps to build up your reserves. You'll have more than you expected. Aquarius and Leo play major roles. You lucky number is 4.

Thursday, April 21 (Moon in Cancer)   A restless mood spurs you to travel, expand horizons, and learn new facts about the world. You'll have a charming companion who talks easily and has plenty to say. Romantic opportunities arise unexpectedly; be prepared. Gemini and Virgo are on the scene.

Friday, April 22 (Moon in Cancer)   You'll be torn between the need for settled conditions and continuing urge for adventure. Cultural events and exhibits that accent beauty, design, decorating or music could be among your far-flung activities. Be in contact with a family member. Your lucky number is 6.

Saturday, April 23 (Moon in Cancer to Leo 9:34 a.m.)   Puzzlement about parent or authority figure will decrease if you listen to the story behind the scenes. Your sense of compassion for others is strong—you'll delve into a mystery and can come up with the right answers. Pisces and Virgo play key roles.

Sunday, April 24 (Moon in Leo)   Rewards for past efforts begin to materialize. You'll feel plenty of pressure, but will understand that the assumption of a leadership role is necessary. Your standing in the community, prestige, and love from others is on the increase. For luck, try number 8.

Monday, April 25 (Moon in Leo to Virgo 10:16 p.m.)   An element of completion and change surrounds your career and wishes about your future. Burdensome chores are about to be finished, leaving more room for creative activities. Don't allow one who may be a "false friend" to steer you. Look for objective advice.

Tuesday, April 26 (Moon in Virgo)   Dare to dream large dreams! You'll succeed through originality, bravery, and an entirely new path. Someone who was just a pal may be seen in a striking new light, possibly quite romantic. Attend a social event and circulate. Learn from a dynamic Leo.

Wednesday, April 27 (Moon in Virgo)   Don't make a move until you clear up indecision over two possible paths. Your intuition is accented; if you listen to "the still, small voice within," you'll be guided in a reassuring way. Surround yourself with supportive, caring individuals. Your lucky number is 2.

Thursday, April 28 (Moon in Virgo to Libra 10:37 a.m.)   Fears and doubts can be quickly cleared up if you accent your sense of humor. A good laugh will clear the air. Restrictions will seem less unpleasant if you dig into a fascinating subject, improving your mind as well as temper. Sagittarius and Gemini people play roles.

Friday, April 29 (Moon in Libra)   Details of vital project cannot be entrusted to another—you must deal with these yourself. Cut yourself off from distracting contacts and pour your energies into problem-solving. You'll win through plain old-fashioned work. Your lucky number is 4.

Saturday, April 30 (Moon in Libra to Scorpio 8:39 a.m.)   The emphasis is on personality, appearance and self-expression. You're surging into a high lunar cycle with a restless urge to expand activities and open lines of communication. Dress sharply; be aware of a member of the opposite sex who has romance in mind.

MAY 1988

Sunday, May 1 (Moon in Scorpio)   This will be a time of testing and discipline. Follow through on good intentions regarding health, weight, diet or nutrition programs. Be patient but thorough. Carelessness now can only lead to disappointment later. Associate with solid citizens.

Monday, May 2 (Moon in Scorpio)   You'll feel new sense of personal freedom and desire to experiment, explore, and meet new people. Trust your first impressions; put across ideas. You'll meet a smooth conversationalist who finds you fascinating and wants to hear more. Your lucky number is 5.

Tuesday, May 3 (Moon in Scorpio to Sagittarius 3:52 a.m.)   Changes regarding your residence could be expensive but satisfying. You'll be more attuned to beauty of surroundings and will want to surround yourself with luxuries. Flowers, music, elegance of attire will all seem vitally important. Learn from Libra person.

Wednesday, May 4 (Moon in Sagittarius)   You won't get something for nothing. Beware of a financial scheme that promises same. Place trust in spiritual values rather than material gain to be on safe ground. The element of loneliness is only temporary; use time to yourself for getting to know the real you.

Thursday, May 5 (Moon in Sagittarius to Capricorn 8:54 a.m.)   Halfway measures won't work. Go all the way in making commitments and promises about the

future. Others are ready to help you if you show ade-
quate sense of responsibility and leadership. Make re-
quests, think big. A Capricorn figures prominently.

Friday, May 6 (Moon in Capricorn)   Hold off on
beginning a new project until you have cleared up
details of old business. A relationship that has unnecessarily limited you is about to end. You'll soon be freer
to increase your sphere of influence; ignore a petty
neighbor. Your lucky number is 9.

**Saturday, May 7 (Moon in Capricorn to Aquarius 12:37
p.m.)**   The accent is on love, physical attraction, and
exciting adventure in local area. Invite the object of
your affection to your own abode; create a happy,
spontaneous atmosphere. There's real cause for celebration; you're making a new start that points to
success.

Sunday, May 8 (Moon in Aquarius)   Avoid becoming entangled in triangles, in quarrels or controversies.
You'll be ultra-sensitive to the opinions of others, but
won't win your way by emotional reactions. Play a waiting game, listen to the counsel of a wise family member. Your lucky number is 2.

**Monday, May 9 (Moon in Aquarius to Pisces 3:39
p.m.)**   Your sense of confinement lifts; you'll view
life with greater enjoyment. Accept an invitation leading to sociability, travel and romance. Someone of the
opposite sex likes you for your enthusiasm and freedom-
loving tendencies. Gemini plays a major role.

Tuesday, May 10 (Moon in Pisces)   Routine duties
demand your attention. You may have to sacrifice personal pleasure for responsibility to others, especially to
younger family members. This could be a testing time
when you're given a chance to make up for past errors.
Your lucky number is 4.

Wednesday, May 11 (Moon in Pisces to Aries 6:23 p.m.) Creative ideas will triumph today. You'll benefit from new methods in both work and play. New information about health, nutrition or physical fitness makes life more interesting and full of variety. A romantic prospect sees you in a new light.

Thursday, May 12 (Moon in Aries) Share tasks with one you love or admire. You'll be particularly attuned to artistic projects involving your home or surroundings. Someone with fixed opinions challenges your ideas, but will back down if you use tact and diplomacy. Your lucky number is 6.

Friday, May 13 (Moon in Aries to Taurus 9:22 p.m.) Don't expect too much from a partner, mate or associate. No one is perfect. The element of self-deception surrounds all relationships today because of dreams and fantasies. Look within for answers rather than becoming overly dependent on others.

Saturday, May 14 (Moon in Taurus) Consult an expert about your marital situation. If single, you're ready to make definite commitments. If already married, you're willing to take on an addition to the family. Intensification of a relationship will bring satisfaction. Your lucky number is 8.

Sunday, May 15 (Moon in Taurus) A big project puts you before the public in a dynamic way. Seek gain from advertising, promotion, or publishing. Refuse to be tied to old conditions that limited you unnecessarily. The best advice comes from one with a sharp, aggressive mind and generous heart.

Monday, May 16 (Moon in Taurus to Gemini 1:31 a.m.) A member of the opposite sex will be pleased if you make the "first move." You'll learn new truths from contact on a deep personal level. The element of

ESP will be evident in the way you relate to each other. This person is lucky for you financially *and* emotionally.

Tuesday, May 17 (Moon in Gemini)   Release old worries about debts, bills, budgets. You'll have the opportunity to reassess the situation and come up with new sources of personal security. An older, parent-type person is ready to help you in more than just money. Your lucky number is 2.

Wednesday, May 18 (Moon in Gemini to Cancer 8:05 a.m.)   You'll be stimulated mentally to expand your horizons. Seek persons who write, lecture, teach, or travel widely. You'll be popular at social events because of your bright, hopeful attitude. There's no stopping you unless you take on more than you can handle.

Thursday, May 19 (Moon in Cancer)   It's time to review, revise and reorganize thoughts about your lifestyle. If you've been breaking rules and cutting corners, you may be brought up short. A seminar or class brings you practical information that can make life smoother. Your lucky number is 4.

Friday, May 20 (Moon in Cancer to Leo 5:51 p.m.) Remain flexible; exciting developments are on the agenda. Be ready to take a trip in pursuit of information, learning or advancement of your career. You'll meet an intriguing member of the opposite sex who shares many interests and desires with you.

Saturday, May 21 (Moon in Leo)   Tactful handling of an authority figure will clear up a temporary "tempest in a teapot" and bring the harmony you desire. You'll be in public eye because of your special talents. Accept recognition graciously and share rewards with loved ones, family members.

Sunday, May 22 (Moon in Leo)   An aura of secrecy and mystery surrounds you and your activities. Others may not understand your motives today, and could be critical of sources of inspiration. Go your own way— depend on personal intuition. Pisces and Virgo people play key roles.

Monday, May 23 (Moon in Leo to Virgo 6:12 a.m.) Important contacts can be made at a meeting of group or organization. Accept duties entrusted to you with realization that career, prestige, or public standing will be enhanced thereby. Someone you love shows increased devotion. The lucky number is 8.

Tuesday, May 24 (Moon in Virgo) The emphasis is on long-range plans and wishes. Your full potential is about to be unveiled, especially if you show you can win friends and influence people. Charitable, humanitarian projects are favored. Aries, Libra and another Scorpio figure prominently.

Wednesday, May 25 (Moon in Virgo to Libra 6:49 p.m.) Seek a secluded rendezvous for your base of operation. Individualism and originality are highlighted. You'll require more time alone for romantic and creative ventures. Your personal charisma will be a strong drawing card—you can get what you want. Keep secrets.

Thursday, May 26 (Moon in Libra) The accent is on family, karmic past and a lucky hunch that works out in an unusual way. Emotions now are stormier than other people suspect; you'll keep feelings under wraps. An older woman or sensitive Pisces type will show compassion. The lucky number is 2.

Friday, May 27 (Moon in Libra) You'll be able to chase the gloom away with a joke or two. A shadowy situation brightens considerably when you take over. Don't allow a sense of confinement or limitation to keep you from exploring fascinating mental interests. A Sagittarian is in the picture.

Saturday, May 28 (Moon in Libra to Scorpio 5:06 a.m.)　　You'll be in the right place at the right time to overcome a major obstacle. The high lunar cycle coincides with self-discipline and an ability to embark on a rigorous self-improvement program. Don't be sidetracked by fun-loving companions. You have work to do!

Sunday, May 29 (Moon in Scorpio)　　Today's emphasis is on self-expression. You'll be on the go, ready to meet an exciting romantic type who has a "way with words." Be willing to depart from rigid ideas in favor of a more flexible life-style. You can write, speak, teach or travel with extra style and flair.

Monday, May 30 (Moon in Scorpio to Sagittarius 11:57 a.m.)　　The desire to rebeautify your environment is valid. Be willing to spend whatever it takes to create the surroundings that will make you and family members happy. Let others pay their share of expenses, however. Don't saddle yourself with all the burdens. Your lucky number is 6.

Tuesday, May 31 (Moon in Sagittarius)　　Transformation of values may come about through much soul-searching. Get away from the mainstream of events and look within for the answers. Perfection of personal talents should also be high in your list of priorities. Pisces and Virgo figure prominently.

J U N E   1 9 8 8

Wednesday, June 1 (Moon in Sagittarius to Capricorn 3:59 p.m.)　　A change of heart about important matter is indicated. You'll review values, relationships and ideas in long-winded discussions. Be versatile, prepared for travel or a whirl of activity. Someone of the opposite sex is interested in what makes you tick.

Thursday, June 2 (Moon in Capricorn)   The accent is on beauty, stability, and improved conditions at home. Artistic expression is encouraged. Study redecoration schemes or plans for new furnishings. You'll feel responsible for loved ones, perhaps more than you should.

Friday, June 3 (Moon in Capricorn to Aquarius 6:34 p.m.)   Take advantage of quiet time to work on self-improvement. You may feel isolated from others, even in the midst of a crowd. The key is to be alone without feeling lonely—rely on your inner resources. A real estate deal could go through. Your lucky number is 7.

Saturday, June 4 (Moon in Aquarius)   Added responsibilities are piled on your shoulders, but you'll handle them with diligence. A family member with prestigious standing in the community will hand out compliments to you, with possibly more tangible signs of approval, including money.

Sunday, June 5 (Moon in Aquarius to Pisces 9 p.m.) Entertainment plans will revolve around your cultural activities, charitable instincts, or futuristic ideas. In matters of the heart, deal with the big picture. Don't fuss over minor issues. Someone who is alert, aggressive and dynamic plays a key role.

Monday, June 6 (Moon in Pisces)   You'll be in the mood for fun, romance and creativity. Someone with a big heart and theatrical personality is ready to go along with your plans. Love and sex are spotlighted. Now is the time to break away from old-fashioned ways. Your lucky number is 1.

Tuesday, June 7 (Moon in Pisces)   The accent is on security and "playing it safe." You'll need to ponder over new steps recently taken—play a waiting game rather than forcing issues today. Emotions and intuition are particularly powerful; you'll be tuned into one you love.

Wednesday, June 8 (Moon in Pisces to Aries 12:04 a.m.) The employment scene takes on a frantic tone. You'll be busy, easily distracted and restless. Maintain your sense of humor when you feel pressures mounting. You can't be everywhere at once; realize this and take one thing at a time. Your lucky number is 3.

Thursday, June 9 (Moon in Aries) Attend to basic tasks in person and expect a routine kind of day. You may feel closed in or confined, but can gain great satisfaction in sticking to the job until it is done. Your judgment is correct about a co-worker. An Aquarius person plays a major role.

Friday, June 10 (Moon in Aries to Taurus 4:02 a.m.) The accent is on partnerships, marital status and an intensified relationship with someone of the opposite sex. A face-to-face confrontation may be needed to convey real feelings to each other. Don't attempt to rely on a phone call or letter. Count on number 5.

Saturday, June 11 (Moon in Taurus) Your sense of duty comes surging to the forefront. You'll attract those with problems to share. Listen more than you talk—let others come to their own conclusions. A family or marriage situation will benefit from more togetherness. Libra plays a role.

Sunday, June 12 (Moon in Taurus to Gemini 9:14 a.m.) An aura of mystery surrounds a strong physical attachment. You may be frustrated by unfulfilled expectations. Learn the true story before you pass judgment. There is more here than meets the eye. The beauties of nature could be healing force.

Monday, June 13 (Moon in Gemini) This power-play day allows you to make a great financial gain. You'll have the aid and backing of superiors. A loan will go through or promotion be granted. Your success story enlarges to include a love relationship that requires tangible proof of your affections.

Tuesday, June 14 (Moon in Gemini to Cancer 4:19 p.m.) You'll put away old concepts and look for new fields to conquer. Higher education, travel, and other methods of expanding vistas promise much. True potential is about to be seen. Get behind that cause or idea you admire. Your lucky number is 9.

Wednesday, June 15 (Moon in Cancer) This is an excellent day to set out on a trip or vacation. You'll be in high spirits, full of vitality and ready for new scenery. Romance will play a prominent role in your adventures. You'll be glowing with sex appeal. A Leo is somewhere in the scene.

Thursday, June 16 (Moon in Cancer) A journey into the past is on the agenda. You'll relive old days with one who taught you much. Visits to museums, old mansions or other historic sites are favored. Much pleasure can be gained through nostalgia. Cancer plays a major role.

Friday, June 17 (Moon in Cancer to Leo 1:57 a.m.) Social contacts prove valuable to career and advancement today. Your enthusiasm is likely to be a major asset, but don't promise more than you can deliver. You'll go places, do things and seek those with bright, inquisitive minds. Your lucky number is 3.

Saturday, June 18 (Moon in Leo) You can prove yourself to a parental or authority figure who needs reassurance. The key is to follow the rules, take your time, and work with the built-in limitations of your current project. Avoid boredom through a sense of challenge; rewards will be great.

Sunday, June 19 (Moon in Leo to Virgo 2:03 p.m.) You'll gain recognition through creative thinking, writing or expressing yourself in imaginative words. Others will be influenced and follow your leadership. Remain flexible to sudden change of plans or direction. Gemini and Virgo play significant roles.

Monday, June 20 (Moon in Virgo) You'll rediscover old friend by attending a social event. An interest in art, music or home decorating is accented. Ideas you pick up could result in an improvement in a family matter. Your sentimental manner attracts Libra or Taurus. Your lucky number is 6.

Tuesday, June 21 (Moon in Virgo) Romantic dreams are likely to be based on false premises. Examine hopes and desires in light of reality. Are you expecting too much from someone who is vague or confusing in manner? You'll succeed in projects that involve illusion, music or films.

Wednesday, June 22 (Moon in Virgo to Libra 2:57 a.m.) Money matters need confidential handling. Keep a secret that has been entrusted to you by an authority figure. A meeting behind the scenes will be to your advantage; go along with plans suggested. Someone who admires you is getting ready to make a serious move.

Thursday, June 23 (Moon in Libra) Break away from limiting conditions; see new possibilities. A relationship that stifled you is about to terminate. Allow others to carry their own loads rather than remaining overly dependent on you. Aries and Libra figure prominently. The lucky number is 9.

Friday, June 24 (Moon in Libra to Scorpio 1:58 p.m.) An exciting new start is on the agenda. You'll be in the driver's seat, able to name your objective and gain it. In matters of the heart, *you* can make the first move successfully. Others will be receptive to your magnetic personality. Leo plays a key role.

Saturday, June 25 (Moon in Scorpio)   Personal matters will be advanced through playing waiting game. Don't be too anxious to change your plans—even if emotions are in a changeable state. Cooperation with family members is your best bet. An older woman has advice on eating, cooking or health matters.

Sunday, June 26 (Moon in Scorpio to Sagittarius 9:18 p.m.)   Your personal popularity is at a high point. You'll attract admiration, generosity and the offer of a pleasant trip. Put your best foot forward where appearance, grooming or wearing apparel are concerned. You can purchase a fascinating item with a foreign flavor.

Monday, June 27 (Moon in Sagittarius)   Check routine, catch up on details. Be sure bills are paid, your checkbook is balanced and records are up to date. You may feel limited by financial circumstances, but will come out on top if you make shrewd, careful moves with money. Your lucky number is 4.

Tuesday, June 28 (Moon in Sagittarius)   Some of your views undergo a great transformation. Close kin or a neighbor will be influential in helping you see the truth. Be open to a frank discussion and rescheduling of an event. A romantic encounter in local area proves exciting. Gemini plays a role.

Wednesday, June 29 (Moon in Sagittarius to Capricorn 1 a.m.)   Domestic argument does not need to flare up. Curtail trouble before it begins by playing a diplomatic role. Money situation will be better than you expected; reassure those around you. Express yourself in art, design, music and home decorating. Your lucky number is 6.

Thursday, June 30 (Moon in Capricorn)   Put off signing important papers until your mind is more clear. Don't believe everything you are told; someone wants to sell you "a bill of goods." You'll be tempted to envision persons, places and events as you wish they could be. Look at situation realistically.

JULY 1988

Friday, July 1 (Moon in Capricorn to Aquarius 2:30 a.m.) The emphasis is on home, family and preparation for a holiday event. You'll attract the cares of others, get involved in community projects, and be concerned with family security. You're apt to take on much more than you can handle. Go easy.

Saturday, July 2 (Moon in Aquarius) Fears and doubts are groundless. Get away by yourself, if possible, and think things through. This is not a highly social day, unless you are working behind the scenes, sacrificing your own desires for the good of others. A Pisces is on the scene.

Sunday, July 3 (Moon in Aquarius to Pisces 2:33 a.m.) Your past efforts pay dividends where an affair of the heart is concerned. Someone who is loyal, true and devoted proves these qualities to you. You'll find romance escalating, but only if you're willing to make serious pledges about the future. Your lucky number is 8.

Monday, July 4 (Moon in Pisces) Entertainment plans expand to include more persons and places than previously expected. You'll be fed up with limitations, artificial barriers. An appreciation of spectacular displays is on the agenda. Aries and Libra figure prominently.

Tuesday, July 5 (Moon in Pisces to Aries 5:37 a.m.) Utilize creative ideas in the job at hand. New faces, new places are likely to be involved. So is a romantic overture from one who shares your daily tasks. Forget about the status quo—make a dynamic new start. Be ready to accept a leadership role.

Wednesday, July 6 (Moon in Aries)   Don't "make waves" in the employment situation today. A diplomatic approach is called for in spite of the urge to have your own way. Real gains can be made through the influence or advice of a family member. Keep a low profile for a while. For better luck, play number 2.

Thursday, July 7 (Moon in Aries to Taurus 9:27 a.m.)   A partner, mate or associate plays a prominent role as day progresses. You may have to bow to wishes of another, but can do so with humor. Your popularity is on the rise because of your more easygoing attitude. Be ready to go along on an exciting trip.

Friday, July 8 (Moon in Taurus)   You'll be more aware of public demands and wishes. You'll feel confined, limited and "put upon" because you must cater to everyone. Instead of making a break for freedom, attend to fine points of the job at hand. The lucky number is 4.

Saturday, July 9 (Moon in Taurus to Gemini 3:16 p.m.)   Restless curiosity to delve into a fascinating new study drives you to make changes in plans. Be flexible, your partners could still be making demands upon you, especially where money and resources are concerned. A Gemini will be involved in a romantic evening.

Sunday, July 10 (Moon in Gemini)   Ask a family member for what you want; you'll be convincing and effective if you use affectionate, diplomatic speech. Budget matters have to be handled with care; there is likely to be a desire for luxury and extravagance. Your lucky number is 6.

Monday, July 11 (Moon in Gemini to Cancer 11:08 p.m.) The tendency is to be withdrawn, introspective, and more interested in spiritual matters than usual. You can gain great rapport with someone of the opposite sex who is sympathetic and compassionate. Words may not be necessary to express special feelings.

Tuesday, July 12 (Moon in Cancer) The accent is on big business, public appeal and the ability to give a wide audience what they're looking for. Take ideas for special promotions or projects to one in an influential position—this can be your lucky day! Contact a Capricorn.

Wednesday, July 13 (Moon in Cancer) Travel plans may have to be postponed or altered. A close associate who is overly dependent on you could limit your actions unless you clearly put an end to this situation. It's time for more universal, widespread interests. Your best bet is number 9.

Thursday, July 14 (Moon in Cancer to Leo 9:11 a.m.) A dynamic new start will be applauded by one in an authority role. This could be just what you need to boost your ego and bring out your best creativity. Your personal magnetism will be high; that gleam in your eye will not be missed by someone of the opposite sex.

Friday, July 15 (Moon in Leo) You'll be more sensitive today, more likely to pull back from the limelight and let someone else shine. You'll feel more comfortable in a cooperative venture and might choose a parental type to work with. Bide your time; follow your intuition. Your lucky number is 2.

Saturday, July 16 (Moon in Leo to Virgo 9:17 a.m.) A social gathering will give you the opportunity you need to share bright ideas with highly mental types. Literature, travel and world situations are on your mind. Keep a sense of humor if someone disagrees with your strong opinions. Your lucky number is 3.

Sunday, July 17 (Moon in Virgo)   You'll be able to see personal objectives in a clear, practical manner. Make a list of what you want to do and take necessary steps to take you there. Resist the urge to run off to a social outing—you have too much to do if you are to make a new project pay off.

Monday, July 18 (Moon in Virgo)   Romantic wishes play a prominent role on this exciting, variety-filled day. Someone who writes, teaches, or works with words wants to get to know you better. Go along with a sudden change in plans; a local trip is highly favored. Your lucky number is 5.

Tuesday, July 19 (Moon in Virgo to Libra 10:22 a.m.)   Your love nature might be difficult to express today unless you seek out a quiet, private rendezvous. A special dinner, gifts, and other assurances of affection will ease the situation. You can break through barriers and reveal your secret feelings. A Libra is attentive.

Wednesday, July 20 (Moon in Libra)   You'll work from behind the scenes, creating illusions, beauty or inspiration from others. Self-understanding is essential if you expect to make positive use of today's sensitivity. Take time out for meditation and music. For luck, try number 7.

Thursday, July 21 (Moon in Libra to Scorpio 10:13 p.m.)   You'll attract attention with a dynamic, enterprising approach to love, money, and career. No one is likely to take you lightly, or not feel your serious intent. This applies especially to an executive who is ready to listen to your innovative plans.

Friday, July 22 (Moon in Scorpio)   A personal situation arises where you can influence large groups of people. Intensify your efforts at self-expression. Be aware of your appearance; wear red or another bright color that will highlight your magnetic, charismatic personality. Your lucky number is 9.

Saturday, July 23 (Moon in Scorpio)   You're in a high lunar cycle, ready for a romantic encounter. You'll be able to make up your own rules; others will go along with the game. A bighearted outgoing person wants to be closer, but is wary of the Scorpio sting. Let go of old grudges now!

Sunday, July 24 (Moon in Scorpio to Sagittarius 6:42 a.m.)   Play for time, rest on your laurels, consider carefully before making a big purchase or threatening the security of the status quo. See where you are financially—bring your bank balance up to date. A family member may be making demands upon you soon. Your lucky number is 2.

Monday, July 25 (Moon in Sagittarius)   Continue to keep the lid on spending. An optimistic view of the future will cause you to speculate and take risks. You'll also be intent on having a good time, and that could be costly. Be more discriminating in your choice of activities. You can't be everywhere at once.

Tuesday, July 26 (Moon in Sagittarius to Capricorn 11:07 a.m.)   The urge for perfection overtakes you. You'll work diligently to overcome obstacles and finish what you started. Only you can handle the details in a way that pleases *you*. A relative who wants to assist is well-meaning but could present a distraction.

Wednesday, July 27 (Moon in Capricorn)   An unexpected visitor pops in at front door, someone who has many stimulating ideas to discuss. Don't expect any dull moments; letters, phone calls and a romantic prospect keep you on your toes. Jot down a key idea before it escapes. Your lucky number is 5.

Thursday, July 28 (Moon in Capricorn to Aquarius 12:25 p.m.)   You've wanted to improve surroundings at base of operations, and now you have a chance. Consult decorators, contractors, painters, and furniture salespersons. The color scheme you select should be restful and calming on the nerves. Your family will appreciate that fact.

Friday, July 29 (Moon in Aquarius)   This unusual day finds you feeling isolated from loved ones, family members. Unexpected sensitivity causes you to feel picked on when others are not even aware you are upset. Find time to be alone and face secret fears or doubts. You can overcome!

Saturday, July 30 (Moon in Aquarius to Pisces 12:23 p.m.)   You'll be more in step with the world, especially those who are "on the way up" on the social or business ladder. If you were in doubt about a matter of the heart, you come to a powerful decision. Your long-term plans occupy much of your attention. Your lucky number is 8.

Sunday, July 31 (Moon in Pisces)   Romantic impulses will be idealistic, inspiring, leading you to greater feats in the outside world. Entertainment plans bring you in contact with a dynamic, forward-looking personality who raises your consciousness. A cause you believe in can be pushed.

AUGUST 1988

Monday, August 1 (Moon in Pisces to Aries 12:53 a.m.)   Relations with fellow employees will improve if you stop being so sensitive. Critical remarks are *not* being directed at you. Perform duties for the joy of creative activity—you'll be especially good at intensive research. The lucky number is 7.

Tuesday, August 2 (Moon in Aries)   Reaction will be favorable to a business proposition you make. One at the top will understand strong ambitions about getting ahead, and wants to help. Money, prestige and long-range plans are favorable for you. Don't take time out for amusements now!

Wednesday, August 3 (Moon in Aries to Taurus 3:24 p.m.)   Timing is favorable for completing a big project and moving on to other fields. The magnetic appeal of your personality will impress both those at work and at home, leading to large-scale conferences or meetings. Get over a petty grudge. Get lucky with number 9.

Thursday, August 4 (Moon in Taurus)   A romantic adventure could lead to a serious partnership. Don't fall into old habits that led to failure with others in the past. Accent new views, originality and less dogmatic or stubborn opinions. Balance your individuality with your cooperative spirit for best results.

Friday, August 5 (Moon in Taurus to Gemini 8:43 p.m.)   Your intuition will be keen about love and money. You'll be able to help a family member or other close associate to gain greater security. This may call for a revised budget or more thrifty ways. Sugar-coat advice with much affection. Your lucky number is 2.

Saturday, August 6 (Moon in Gemini)   Obligations to others keep you busy, traveling, talking and teaching what you have recently learned. You'll be in the mood to investigate a system of thought that is surrounded with secrecy. Don't be satisfied until you have learned the real story.

Sunday, August 7 (Moon in Gemini)   The emphasis is on money, investments, bank balances and a review of insurance plans. Your eagle eye won't let much get by. Catch errors, see where profit to you can be improved. An Aquarian shows up—don't let this person distract you. Your lucky number is 4.

Monday, August 8 (Moon in Gemini to Cancer 4:52 a.m.)   A letter or phone message from afar contains news that gives you a fresh sense of freedom and adventure. This could include contact with a romantic foreigner. You'll overcome language or cultural barrier to get creative ideas across. A Gemini figures prominently.

Tuesday, August 9 (Moon in Cancer)   The accent is on music, art, beauty and visits to cultural centers. Escort an out-of-towner to local spots of interest. You'll find much that you had overlooked in your own area. A family situation will improve through uplifting activities. Your lucky number is 6.

Wednesday, August 10 (Moon in Cancer to Leo 3:26 p.m.)   An aura of mystery surrounds an authority figure. This person is likely to influence you in way you hadn't expected. You'll be likely to be led astray, however, if you place this person on a pedestal. Listen: No one is perfect! Look within for authentic answers.

Thursday, August 11 (Moon in Leo)   A long-coveted career goal can be won if you set wheels in motion energetically. Be enterprising; see a prestigious person who can help you with money or information. A loved one will be impressed, and is more likely to say "yes" in a romantic situation.

Friday, August 12 (Moon in Leo)   Promotion or advancement is within sight! The new moon sets you off on a fresh direction, but first you must release old ideas that have held you back. Your natural leadership ability is very much in evidence now. An Aries will help. Your lucky number is 9.

Saturday, August 13 (Moon in Leo to Virgo 5:46 a.m.) Interesting developments take place in a friendship. One who was only a pal grows much more serious. You'll be in a fun-loving, outgoing mood, and can pretty much have your way where romance is concerned. Leo and Aquarius figure prominently.

Sunday, August 14 (Moon in Virgo) A family member demands your presence at a social event. Go along with the plans of others, especially an older person to whom you owe much for past favors. You'll be comfortable in the presence of friendly, familiar faces at a celebration. Your lucky number is 2.

Monday, August 15 (Moon in Virgo to Libra 4:52 p.m.) Think positively about dreams and plans. A restless desire to reach beyond your current boundaries may not be satisfied immediately, but there's no need for gloom. You can research educational subjects and learn much for use in the future. A Sagittarian is in picture.

Tuesday, August 16 (Moon in Libra) Much can be accomplished behind the scenes if you stick to a plan. Take one step at a time and plunge into detail work that has piled up. There's no need to feel put upon or sorry for yourself—real rewards are on the way to you. Your lucky number is 4.

Wednesday, August 17 (Moon in Libra) The clever use of your mind is accented. You'll produce original ideas with ease, especially in a literary or teaching venture. Secret information comes to you, possibly through a romantic member of the opposite sex who wants to impress you. Gemini plays a key role.

Thursday, August 18 (Moon in Libra to Scorpio 5:12 a.m.)　　Your emphasis is on your personality, appearance, and manner of meeting and greeting others. *Do* be concerned with how you look, no matter how much pressure is on you to solve a family situation. A loved one will say you look positively radiant. Your lucky number is 5.

Friday, August 19 (Moon in Scorpio)　　Chances are you will seem aloof, self-absorbed or difficult to get to know. Realize that a prospective friend is intrigued by your air of mystery and wants very much to discover "the real you." Allow this person to come closer and share your dreams.

Saturday, August 20 (Moon in Scorpio to Sagittarius 2:55 p.m.)　　Your business sense is excellent—you can pull off a big deal and smile all the way to the bank. A combination of no-nonsense personality and strong capabilities is unbeatable. You'll impress those who are prospective customers or clients. Your lucky number is 8.

Sunday, August 21 (Moon in Sagittarius)　　Your generosity knows no bounds. You'll want to help those in need, even if they're a world away from you. Be discriminating in sharing resources, however. Someone who depends on you too much, and is weakened thereby, needs to stand on own two feet.

Monday, August 22 (Moon in Sagittarius to Capricorn 8:49 p.m.)　　Don't be afraid to follow your original impulse to branch off into daring new ventures, especially on the local level. Self-expression of all kinds is highly favored. Close kin, neighbors and friends are involved. So is a Leo. Your lucky number is 1.

Tuesday, August 23 (Moon in Capricorn)　　Twosome makes better sense than going it alone. This applies especially to projects where you write, travel locally or find answers to emotional perplexity. Rely on your intuition more than reason and common sense. A Cancer plays a major role.

Wednesday, August 24 (Moon in Capricorn to Aquarius 11:05 p.m.)   You'll be the life of every party or social get-together. The tendency will be to move fast, talk much, and take on more than you can possibly handle. Your willingness to say what you really think may be refreshing, but not to everyone. Count on number 3.

Thursday, August 25 (Moon in Aquarius)   The home base requires your undivided attention. Tend to repairs, replacements, and reorganization of facts and figures. You'll be tempted to cut corners or throw out the rule book—realize this is very foolish. Family security and your own is at stake.

Friday, August 26 (Moon in Aquarius to Pisces 11:01 p.m.)   The sense of confinement lifts. You'll be in an experimental mood, ready to change ideas about the family life-style. Someone with a rigid belief structure is swinging over to a modern viewpoint. This could be cause for a celebration or brief trip. The lucky number is 5.

Saturday, August 27 (Moon in Pisces)   A summertime festivity will involve the entire family. A reunion with those long out of the picture is a definite possibility. Make elaborate plans for entertainment, including music, dancing, and performances by local talent. Libra and Taurus play roles.

Sunday, August 28 (Moon in Pisces to Aries 10:29 p.m.)   The full moon finds you in a dreamy, expectant mood, ready for romance, adventures and sharing of sentimental feelings. As long as you are completely realistic about the situation, you won't be disappointed.

229

Are you merely in love with love? Your lucky number is 7.

Monday, August 29 (Moon in Aries)   The accent is on work, health, dependents and obligations to help others. Those who share your daily concerns are ready to look to you to get them organized. You'll assume a leadership role very naturally, even without being asked. A Capricorn is in the picture.

Tuesday, August 30 (Moon in Aries to Taurus 11:22 p.m.)   Your sphere of personal influence increases. You'll meet more people through your daily work and will see some of them in a brand-new light. It's time to let go of the "chip on your shoulder" and offer to forgive and forget. Others respond in kind. The lucky number is 9.

Wednesday, August 31 (Moon in Taurus)   New ideas about partnerships may shock some, but will seem only natural to you. You'll be full of zest and enthusiasm to unleash creative powers. Consider the effect on others before you proceed. A proud dramatic individual wants more of your attention—give it!

SEPTEMBER 1988

Thursday, September 1 (Moon in Taurus)   Expect an intensified relationship with a loyal, serious-minded member of the opposite sex. This person is connected with business, but wants to see you in a more personal situation. You'll be attracted by chance to get ahead or share glory. The lucky number is 8.

Friday, September 2 (Moon in Taurus to Gemini 3:11 a.m.)   Resources you had expected to share may not materialize. The reason is that incompatible temperaments are involved. You'll do better in an entirely new situation, both in love and money. Enlarge your vision and see new possibilities. An Aries plays a key role.

Saturday, September 3 (Moon in Gemini)   Someone you meet now presents a real challenge, requiring that you undergo transformation. Dig deep for answers concerning an alliance; consider the extent of your physical attraction. You'll come up with original answers and solutions. Your lucky number is 1.

Sunday, September 4 (Moon in Gemini to Cancer 10:37 a.m.)   This quiet, peaceful day gives you a chance to ponder spiritual truths. A powerful dream from last night could still be source of influence. The desire to return to your past life-style or situation could be based on nostalgia. Enjoy memories; then come back to the present.

Monday, September 5 (Moon in Cancer)   Tackle one thing at a time; don't have too many irons in the fire. You'll want to study, travel, and spread a personal message in fiery discussions. Consolidate your energies and concentrate on one valid goal. You could publish something. Your lucky number is 3.

Tuesday, September 6 (Moon in Cancer to Leo 9:14 p.m.)   A practical approach to your career is favored. Be shrewd and observant about opportunities open for advancement. Read through ads, consult experts, and take note of bulletin boards. The no-nonsense approach will pay off. Aquarius and Leo are in the picture.

Wednesday, September 7 (Moon in Leo)   Focus on communication, including writing, speaking and teaching. You'll gain recognition for innovative ideas, exciting discoveries or freshly uncovered information. Don't be fearful of change—strike while the iron is hot. You'll win! The lucky number is 5.

Thursday, September 8 (Moon in Leo)   Don't allow a family fracas to affect your reputation. Put an end to wrangling even before it begins. An adjustment in schedule, time spent with loved ones, or changes in your physical layout will pay dividends in greater harmony. Libra has ideas about redecorating.

Friday, September 9 (Moon in Leo to Virgo 9:48 a.m.)   You'll want to pass by social events to enjoy beauties of out-of-doors and nature. Take along sympathetic pal who can understand the extrasensitive mood you're in. You'll drop sophomoric desires in favor of a more mature attitude. The lucky number is 7.

Saturday, September 10 (Moon in Virgo)   The new moon provides a fresh, invigorating start. You'll see ambitions in a new light, realizing how you can build upon past efforts to assure future success. Be serious about a love relationship; give commitments asked for. Capricorn and Cancer are on the scene.

Sunday, September 11 (Moon in Virgo to Libra 10:51 p.m.)   The accent is on giving rather than receiving. An altruistic attitude is favored, especially in a group situation. Say "yes" to those who ask for valid donations—you'll be helping a worthy cause. Rewards will come back to you in the future. Your lucky number is 9.

Monday, September 12 (Moon in Libra)   You'll be impatient for new directions, but limited by old fears and self-doubts. If you cannot yet make an impression on the outside world, spend time behind the scenes working on a creative project that reflects the real you. A Leo provides the ideal inspiration.

Tuesday, September 13 (Moon in Libra)   Your intuition is your greatest asset today. You'll absorb facts, information, and feelings of others from the environment in an almost psychic way. Your aggressive urges are not strong; you'll desire protection, nurturance and love. For luck, try number 2.

Wednesday, September 14 (Moon in Libra to Scorpio 11:07 a.m.)   Your popularity and self-assurance surge upward as the day progresses. The high lunar cycle suggests that you can win friends and influence people. Seek out social situations; dress sharply; display your wit, intelligence and sense of humor. Be ready for applause!

Thursday, September 15 (Moon in Scorpio)   Now is the time to focus on personal habits, weight, and physical conditions. You'll have the self-discipline to carry through on a vigorous program. Follow instructions, rules and regulations to the letter for best results. Don't give up! Number 4 brings success.

Friday, September 16 (Moon in Scorpio to Sagittarius 9:25 p.m.)   Statements you make today could have a gigantic effect on your personal future. Remain open to romance, change, variety and a chance for a trip to a local spot of interest. A valuable gift could be yours in an encounter with a member of the opposite sex. Enjoy!

Saturday, September 17 (Moon in Sagittarius)   A luxury item for the home will make a real difference in the harmony of the atmosphere. Don't count the cost if the happiness of one you love is involved. Shop for gourmet goodies, special sweets and colorful flowers. Consideration will pay off. Your lucky number is 6.

Sunday, September 18 (Moon in Sagittarius)   You won't get something for nothing. The offer of an item that sounds too good to be true is just that. Count your change; double-check facts and figures. You'll be in a dreamy, idealistic mood that others may take advantage of. A Pisces is on *your* side.

Monday, September 19 (Moon in Sagittarius to Capricorn 4:45 a.m.)   This power-play day gives you chance to finalize contracts, big deals and shake hands on valid offers. Close kin, neighbors and others close to you will lend support and encouraging words. An executive follows through on a previous promise. Your lucky number is 8.

Tuesday, September 20 (Moon in Capricorn) The urge to expand your horizons, spread influence and break free of old bonds is felt strongly. In taking a "giant step" don't overlook old pals or associates who shared your daily rounds. This can be a real challenge! Aries and Libra figure prominently.

Wednesday, September 21 (Moon in Capricorn to Aquarius 8:43 a.m.) A family member helps you to see a more original way of doing things. Listen to good advice; then go into action! Make a decision about love, marriage and residence. Add bright touches to your surroundings; plan your home entertainment. Leo plays a key role. The lucky number is 1.

Thursday, September 22 (Moon in Aquarius) Save time and energy today; bypass unnecessary activity. You'll have opportunity to make contact with persons close to you, including a parent or parental figure. The urge for security will motivate you to put away resources for a future "rainy day."

Friday, September 23 (Moon in Aquarius to Pisces 9:51 a.m.) Look for the "silver lining." Big hopes surround special occasion and an affair of the heart. A fresh burst of energy and enthusiasm will set you off on a round of socializing, travel, or pursuit of entertainment. A Sagittarian is in the picture. Your lucky number is 3.

Saturday, September 24 (Moon in Pisces) A creative project requires extreme practicality. Set down ideas in a logical sequence; follow through on inspirations that pop into yuor mind. You may be tempted to run away from self-imposed tasks, but would be sorry later. An Aquarius plays a role.

Sunday, September 25 (Moon in Pisces to Aries 9:29 a.m.)   One who comes to you for aid can best be helped through good advice. A transformation of ideas is needed before this person can stand on own two feet. The tension and excitement of a full moon may be part of the problem. Take care of your health. The lucky number is 5.

Monday, September 26 (Moon in Aries)   Your daily routine becomes more stable and settled. Keep calm, even if a co-worker or family member causes a temporary tempest in a teapot. Your own need for peace and harmony will motivate you to use tact and diplomacy in handling personal relationships.

Tuesday, September 27 (Moon in Aries to Taurus 9:29 a.m.)   The accent is on partnerships, marital status and legal maneuvers. Don't believe everything you hear; someone who is rather vague and uncertain could mislead you by not telling the entire story. Reserve your judgment; obtain more details. Your lucky number is 7.

Wednesday, September 28 (Moon in Taurus)   You'll gain greater prestige, money and recognition through association with one who knows the score. Take advantage of favorable business contacts, especially with those who are loyal and trustworthy. Capricorn and Cancer play major roles.

Thursday, September 29 (Moon in Taurus to Gemini 11:43 a.m.)   A pioneering type bursts on the scene, full of forward-looking ideas. Don't allow limited thinking to hold you back from sharing a project that could be highly profitable for you both. Dreams *can* be transformed into reality! The lucky number is 9.

Friday, September 30 (Moon in Gemini)   A romance intensifies as feelings mount. You'll be caught up in emotions deeper than you had expected. New ways of relating to each other are needed; share dreams and fancies. You'll be full of original ideas—express them. Leo could be in the picture.

OCTOBER 1988

Saturday, October 1 (Moon in Gemini to Cancer 5:39 p.m.)   Now is the time for big financial project. You could be winner in business deal, purchase or contest. Enlarge your expectations—don't be satisfied with petty gains. You'll reach beyond current limitations. Let go of possessions no longer of value to you.

Sunday, October 2 (Moon in Cancer)   Get set for travel, learning and expansion of horizons. Visit places you've never been before, meet new people with bold ideas. A romantic member of the opposite sex will be delighted to share your thoughts and feelings on the trip. Your lucky number is 1.

Monday, October 3 (Moon in Cancer)   A message from afar brings you in touch again with one who figured prominently in your past. Take advantage of this opportunity to share old memories, plus news of recent events. You'll receive a bit of advice; be receptive, especially to an older, parental type.

Tuesday, October 4 (Moon in Cancer to Leo 3:31 a.m.)   A dynamic career move can be made through a recent social contact. Opportunities exist in advertising, publishing, broadcasting or other fields where you spread ideas and influence many. Your personal popularity is at a high point; take advantage. Your lucky number is 3.

Wednesday, October 5 (Moon in Leo)   Concentrate on detail work that has piled up. You'll impress a superior by following through in a responsible manner in spite of temptations to split from scene. Follow rules and regulations; don't cut corners. An Aquarian figures prominently.

Thursday, October 6 (Moon in Leo to Virgo 4:01 p.m.) The accent is on communication, messages, ideas that gain favor with persons at the top of the ladder. Promote yourself in your career. If ready for a change, send out resumes, make phone calls and contact employment agencies. Do it now! The lucky number is 5.

Friday, October 7 (Moon in Virgo) A family celebration could be cause for many gifts and much sentiment. Beautify your surroundings, buy flowers, arrange for music and gourmet dining fare. You'll win the heart of one who was somewhat estranged recently. Libra and Taurus play prominent parts.

Saturday, October 8 (Moon in Virgo) Dreams and wishes tend to be fanciful, possibly out of reach. Don't feel sorry for yourself if expectations about a special person are not fulfilled to the letter. Take a walk and enjoy the beauties of nature with a calm, sympathetic friend. Your lucky number is 7.

Sunday, October 9 (Moon in Virgo to Libra 5:03 a.m.) Look behind the scenes for answers. An older, more experienced person will help you with advice, financial backing or other support. You'll gain through past efforts and reputation you have earned for stability. Self-doubts have no place in the picture!

Monday, October 10 (Moon in Libra) You'll see more clearly why it's necessary to break away from old conditions now. A burden that you have been carrying is not legitimately yours; don't hamper another who can walk on own two feet. An Aries will tell it like it is. The lucky number is 9.

Tuesday, October 11 (Moon in Libra to Scorpio 4:58 p.m.) Life takes on a new glow and sense of excitement. You'll surge into a high lunar cycle, giving you more control of your own life. Your appearance could undergo some dramatic change, either through hairstyle, clothes, or other means. A Leo will find you fascinating!

Wednesday, October 12 (Moon in Scorpio) The accent is on the gentler side of your nature. You'll gain through tuning into the needs and wants of others, really listening to what they're saying to you. It's essential to watch your weight right now—don't eat for emotional reasons. Your lucky number is 2.

Thursday, October 13 (Moon in Scorpio) The accent is on social life, expansion and travel. Experiment with new styles, both in clothing and self-expression. You'll meet an exciting foreigner who likes your sense of humor. Romance tends to be lighthearted, not very serious or committed.

Friday, October 14 (Moon in Scorpio to Sagittarius 2:58 a.m.) Plug loopholes where spending is concerned. Make sure plans and aspirations are solid rather than flimsy. You can improve credit, money position, and bank account through careful examination of details. Stick to the job at hand. Your lucky number is 4.

Saturday, October 15 (Moon in Sagittarius) You'll gain through a meaningful alliance. A member of the opposite sex wants to share thoughts, resources and time. Discover how you can combine forces in a money-making venture. Expect change, travel and variety as the romantic scenario unfolds. Gemini plays a key role.

Sunday, October 16 (Moon in Sagittarius to Capricorn 10:44 a.m.) A luxury purchase for home or family will bring cries of delight. Indulge yourself and those you love in celebration that includes music, gourmet fare and homestyle entertainment. Slight misunderstanding will be quickly settled. Your lucky number is 6.

Monday, October 17 (Moon in Capricorn)   The accent is on working behind the scenes, keeping ideas secret, and maintaining a low profile. Use intuition "to read between the lines" in an important communication. All is not as it seems on the surface. Pisces and Virgo figure prominently.

Tuesday, October 18 (Moon in Capricorn to Aquarius 4:05 p.m.)   A power play wins you support in your local neighborhood and among family members. Show you are ready to take on extra duties to back up commitments made to those you love. Money, prestige and other rewards of ambition are on the way. The lucky number is 8.

Wednesday, October 19 (Moon in Aquarius)   Finish projects, release your past, especially where property rights are concerned. It's time to expand past limitations imposed upon you when younger. Interests beyond the four walls of your home are strongly favored. Aries and Libra play key roles.

Thursday, October 20 (Moon in Aquarius to Pisces 6:58 p.m.)   Be daring in dress and manner. A dynamic member of the opposite sex wants to know you better and can be the source of much pleasure and entertainment. You'll be lucky in love, speculation or games of chance. Stick with Leo and the number 1.

Friday, October 21 (Moon in Pisces)   A younger family member comes to you with source of genuine concern. You can soothe foolish fears and point out a more productive path. Old-fashioned forms of social life or recreation will possess unique appeal. A Cancer is in the picture.

Saturday, October 22 (Moon in Pisces to Aries 7:59 p.m.) Your energies may be scattered, making chores difficult to complete until later in the day. Get socializing out of the way early, meet with those who share your daily concerns and plan exciting trip. You'll be highly popular today. Your lucky number is 3.

Sunday, October 23 (Moon in Aries) The sense of confinement will lift when duties to others have been completed. Any attempt to cut corners or evade responsibility is not advised. You'll earn a glow of satisfaction for a job well done if you stick to tasks until they are completed. An Aquarius takes notice.

Monday, October 24 (Moon in Aries to Taurus 8:22 p.m.) Better communication with the key person in your life leads to a profitable, productive endeavor. The writing project could be on the agenda; a clever partner helps you express unique ideas. Prepare for travel, change, variety. Your lucky number is 5.

Tuesday, October 25 (Moon in Taurus) The emphasis is on togetherness, companionship, love and loyalty. Invite a partner, mate or associate to share your deepest feelings; listen more than you talk. You'll be able to kiss and make up with one who was on the outs. A domestic type figures prominently.

Wednesday, October 26 (Moon in Taurus to Gemini 9:55 p.m.) The sense of compassion and sympathy for others is strong. Don't allow a subtle type to take advantage of your good nature. You may not be seeing persons of the opposite sex too clearly because of need to seek ideal person. Wake up! Your lucky number is 7.

Thursday, October 27 (Moon in Gemini) Business and money prospects are better than expected. You'll attract those who want to invest in you and your talents. The opportunity to go into business for yourself should be seriously considered. Your self-

240

confidence is high, drawing an eligible member of opposite sex.

Friday, October 28 (Moon in Gemini)   Take inventory, reassess the situation. A chance exists to let go of items you no longer need—another is more than willing to buy. You'll be magnetic, generous, bighearted. An Aries can help you to transform dreams into reality. The lucky number is 9.

Saturday, October 29 (Moon in Gemini to Cancer 5:28 a.m.)   The feeling of independence is strong, leading you to seek answers and opportunities at a distance. A long journey, educational improvement or philosophical discussion could expand your outlook immensely. Expect exciting new faces, places and situations.

Sunday, October 30 (Moon in Cancer)   A nostalgic journey takes you down "memory lane." You'll meet again someone who taught or inspired you in the past. Be considerate of a family member who wants to tag along on your activities. You can set a good example for someone younger. Your lucky number is 2.

Monday, October 31 (Moon in Cancer to Leo 11:03 a.m.)   Keep your sense of humor if you feel you must reform the world today. The tendency is to take on more than you can handle, especially in far-flung interests and issues. Your reputation rests upon being taken seriously by others; don't scatter forces wildly!

NOVEMBER 1988

Tuesday, November 1 (Moon in Leo)   Your sex appeal could be the key factor in winning promotion in career. Someone in a position of authority is aware of your charms, but also of other assets. You'll receive the nod of approval for bright, forward-looking ideas and creativity. Your lucky number is 1.

Wednesday, November 2 (Moon in Leo to Virgo 11:02 p.m.) An older person has sage advice about reputation. Keep a low profile, be ready to cooperate and establish a firm base for security. You may make headway slowly if you vacillate or become overly emotional. Be diplomatic; don't force issues!

Thursday, November 3 (Moon in Virgo) You'll break out of an emotional rut in a burst of optimism and good cheer. Your hopes and wishes may exceed what is legitimately possible, however. Accept a social invitation—someone you meet will share interests in a fascinating subject. Your lucky number is 3.

Friday, November 4 (Moon in Virgo) Finish what you have started. A practical project needs to be completed in spite of the lure of fun and games. A pal who wants to help doesn't know the details as you do; handle it yourself. You'll feel better as you check off items on your list.

Saturday, November 5 (Moon in Virgo to Libra 12:04 p.m.) Attention from a member of the opposite sex puts you in a delightful mood early in the day. Romantic dreams swim in your head; you'll seek the privacy of secluded rendezvous for dinner and dancing. Share those secrets you've been saving up so long. Your lucky number is 5.

Sunday, November 6 (Moon in Libra) You'll become the counselor behind the scenes to family members and others close to you. Realize that you can listen, but only the other person can actually solve the situation. Supportive attention and affection help most. Virgo plays a key role.

Monday, November 7 (Moon in Libra to Scorpio 11:46 p.m.) You'll wish you had the day off to get away by yourself and think. Wherever you are, play the waiting

242

game; be sensitive to moods of others, but stay clear of interference. Your sense of personal isolation will soon lift; make the best of it. Your lucky number is 7.

Tuesday, November 8 (Moon in Scorpio) A surge of power and vitality lift you into a more practical, enterprising sphere of action. The business or romantic situation will go just the way you want it to. The key is to accent loyalty, devotion, and responsibility. Capricorn and Cancer are in the picture.

Wednesday, November 9 (Moon in Scorpio) Words you speak today will have a lasting impact on a large number of people. Utilize personal magnetism for a good cause, including expansion of your own constructive endeavors. Pay attention to high principles; don't settle for less. Your lucky number is 9.

Thursday, November 10 (Moon in Scorpio to Sagittarius 9:06 a.m.) Cash in on the high lunar cycle. You'll be in the driver's seat in romantic situations, money affairs or promotion of original ideas. Bold moves bring you your heart's desires. Wear bright colors, break free of status quo, make first move. Leo admires you.

Friday, November 11 (Moon in Sagittarius) Your mind will be on family, security, and a round-about way of obtaining your wishes. Discuss budget, savings, and solid investments with one who has earned your respect. An intuitive hunch about money or contest could be quite valid—go for it! Count on number 2.

Saturday, November 12 (Moon in Sagittarius to Capricorn 4:12 p.m.) Your local area becomes the scene of much activity, excitement, and socializing. You may feel impatient at the narrow interests of some in your family or neighborhood, but an upbeat mood will keep you relating harmoniously to all. Seek the company of a bright Sagittarian.

Sunday, November 13 (Moon in Capricorn)   A feeling of being closed in provides the spark to get a personal project completed. Attend to clearing up the odds and ends of writing, correspondence and other communications. A close relative thinks you have been aloof. The lucky number is 4.

Monday, November 14 (Moon in Capricorn to Aquarius 9:36 p.m.)   You'll be sick of rules, regulations and other standards set down by family members or daily associates. Be brave enough to make daring changes in your life-style, ideas and relationships. A Gemini wants to talk to you; open lines of communication.

Tuesday, November 15 (Moon in Aquarius)   Your artistic urges are stimulated by your surroundings. You'll be in the mood to redecorate, freshen up or otherwise improve appearance of the home or office. Later a warm fire and affectionate companionship sets the scene for romantic feelings. Your lucky number is 6.

Wednesday, November 16 (Moon in Aquarius)   A puzzling situation at your base of operations could be the source of discomfort—if you let it. Choose instead to learn the story behind the scenes and ferret out secrets of a loved one who is upset. Be realistic about what you hear; don't expect perfection from anyone.

Thursday, November 17 (Moon in Aquarius to Pisces 1:34 a.m.)   There's no halfway measures where love is concerned. You'll be deeply involved or not at all. The problem is you may have to come up with a definite commitment that requires really serious intent. A tough decision may have to be made. Your lucky number is 8.

Friday, November 18 (Moon in Pisces)   The accent is on entertainment, social situations and recreation. If you're bored with some activities on your upcoming schedule, be ready to evaluate what you want to eliminate. An enlarged vision about the future could bring transformed views about groups and associations.

Saturday, November 19 (Moon in Pisces to Aries 4:12 a.m.) You'll need to insert a touch of drama in your obligations and chores today in order to get through them. Be original, creative, think of alternate methods. Make a party out of tasks, inviting others to join you. Others will be attracted. Your lucky number is 1.

Sunday, November 20 (Moon in Aries) Keep a low profile, go along with the wishes of those you hold dear. Focus on health situations that can be aided by more rest and relaxation. You'll want familiar faces around you, offering plenty of nurturing and attention to your moods. An older woman plays a role.

Monday, November 21 (Moon in Aries to Taurus 6:02 a.m.) Pay attention to public relations, advertising and reaching as many people as possible. A light touch of humor will help. You have a positive message to share. A social occasion may require travel and be costly; don't overdo! The lucky number is 3.

Tuesday, November 22 (Moon in Taurus) The emphasis is on handling a partnership in a practical, no-nonsense way. Be willing to accept rules, regulations and limitations in interactions. Exciting moments may be few, but you'll feel grateful that you've worked things out together smoothly.

Wednesday, November 23 (Moon in Taurus to Gemini 8:12 a.m.) The pace of life picks up; a physical relationship grows deeper and more intense. The key is to talk over differences, then be willing to change tactics, if necessary. Probe for psychological attitudes. Spend money on a change of scene. Your lucky number is 5.

Thursday, November 24 (Moon in Gemini) A family gathering will be peaceful, loving, and abundant with the good things of life. Share resources freely with family members who have less than you. This includes a stubborn person whom you sometimes avoid. Libra and Taurus are in the picture.

Friday, November 25 (Moon in Gemini to Cancer 12:19 p.m.) Grab an opportunity to "get away from it all." A visit to a quiet retreat will do wonders for your spirits. Don't worry about the cost—you need exposure to the beauties of nature far away from the crowds. A Pisces is in the picture. Your lucky number is 7.

Saturday, November 26 (Moon in Cancer) The accent is on serious intentions, long-range plans. Sit down with an older, experienced person and map future strategy in your career. You may find you need to take a class or two to prepare yourself for a more advanced position. A loved one will cheer you on!

Sunday, November 27 (Moon in Cancer to Leo 7:52 p.m.) You'll be in the limelight for generosity and humanitarian impulses. Someone you help will let everyone know about good deeds. Keep the higher good in mind rather than your own personal glory—seek understanding; get in touch with the "universal mind." Your lucky number is 9.

Monday, November 28 (Moon in Leo) You'll spot new a trend in the world about you, and can capitalize on this. Open your mind to new endeavors, originality and independence. Then get in touch with a dynamic executive who can back you in an entrepreneurial venture. You can sell your ideas!

Tuesday, November 29 (Moon in Leo) You'll need time out to consider all angles of a situation carefully. Avoid direct confrontations, especially with persons in authority roles. Right now, you may be overly emotional, too tied up with past issues to see straight. Your lucky number is 2.

Wednesday, November 30 (Moon in Leo to Virgo 7 a.m.)
The accent is on a high-flying social life and optimism
that soars above most obstacles. You'll be thinking big
where life, love, and friendship are concerned. The
problem is you may trip over a minor detail. A foreign
friend challenges you to reconstruct your views.

DECEMBER 1988

Thursday, December 1 (Moon in Virgo)   Reserve
time for a family get-together. Listen closely to the
hopes and desires of loved ones. You'll receive valuable
tips about what type of gifts to buy. A conversation
about old times will reveal how much each one of you
means to the other.

**Friday, December 2 (Moon in Virgo to Libra 7:56
p.m.)**   A sudden spurt of energy pushes you to take
on more than you can handle. A promise you have
made to a friend may not be fulfilled because of lack of
time. You'll want to go places and do things, most of
them social or entertaining. The lucky number is 3.

Saturday, December 3 (Moon in Libra)   Routine
matters will absorb much of your day. You may have to
forego social plans this evening in order to catch up
with duties and obligations. The sense of confinement
and limitations is only temporary. You're building the
foundation for more secure future.

Sunday, December 4 (Moon in Libra)   An exciting
drama takes place behind the scenes. You'll hear the
romantic words you've wanted to hear from someone
who matters. Barriers that have existed will break down,
enabling this person to see you in clearer, brighter
light. Your lucky number is 5.

**Monday, December 5 (Moon in Libra to Scorpio 7:51
a.m.)**   Hidden facts will be revealed, allowing you to

emerge from behind the scenes. A sense of duty pushes you to take responsibility for chores that are not rightly yours. Think about your own appearance; have you gotten "run down at the heels?" Spend time on grooming.

Tuesday, December 6 (Moon in Scorpio)   You'll be on a "spiritual high," all wrapped up in ideals, beauty and inspiration. Enjoy the moment, but don't bank the future on promises made to you today. Give for the joy of giving, without thought of return. A Pisces is in picture. So is number 7.

Wednesday, December 7 (Moon in Scorpio to Sagittarius 4:55 p.m.)   An enterprising attitude in dealing with a powerful person puts you in leadership role. You'll cash in financially on a solid proposition endorsed by solid citizen. Take the long-range view in investments or handling of money. Capricorn and Cancer people play key roles.

Thursday, December 8 (Moon in Sagittarius)   Clean out closets, drawers and cupboards. Give away what you don't want or need. You'll make way for new prosperity by clearing out deadwood from past. Consider too whether you're hanging on to attitudes that are not healthy. Your lucky number is 9.

Friday, December 9 (Moon in Sagittarius to Capricorn 11:07 p.m.)   Put your money on original ideas! A flair for creative, dramatic projects gains you an audience, including a Leo who likes the way you operate. Investment in a bright new outfit will dazzle onlookers. Don't be afraid to set new fashions and trends.

Saturday, December 10 (Moon in Capricorn)   Send a sentimental note to someone you'll never forget. Your ability to express emotions in affectionate manner is at a high point. All correspondence and messages will contain special a personal accent. Relatives play a key role in plans today. Your lucky number is 2.

Sunday, December 11 (Moon in Capricorn)   The accent is on distant places, foreign foods and fashions, and an outgoing, highly sociable attitude. A visit to an ethnic restaurant with local folk would provide that touch of "something different" you require today. A Sagittarius or Gemini offers good conversation.

Monday, December 12 (Moon in Capricorn to Aquarius 3:25 a.m.)   You may feel closed in by Monday blues. Keep plugging away at tasks in spite of inner resistance; you'll soon fall into a groove that's comfortable and rewarding. A real estate deal requires extra close scrutiny. Be aware of the fine points. Your lucky number is 4.

Tuesday, December 13 (Moon in Aquarius)   A romantic scenario unfolds in your domestic atmosphere. Dinner for two could evolve into a much closer tête-à-tête. Get together for an interesting discussion of mutual interest; then see what develops. You'll be tuned into ideas, five senses and adventure.

Wednesday, December 14 (Moon in Aquarius to Pisces 6:53 a.m.)   Focus on the needs and desires of younger family members. Home-oriented entertainment is favored. Emphasize also creative projects that bring out your artistic side; your home will be beautified in the process. Consult a Libra for decorating tips. Your lucky number is 6.

Thursday, December 15 (Moon in Pisces)   An affair of the heart is surrounded by glamour, romance, but also a touch of unreality. You'll be a "pushover" for sentimental story or plea for special consideration. Enjoy magical moments but don't be surprised if a relationship is not built on firm ground.

Friday, December 16 (Moon in Pisces to Aries 10:03 a.m.)   A speculative venture is favored. You'll be shrewd enough to figure the odds and put money on a "sure thing." Your business sense is excellent now; so is luck in love and romance. Capricorn and Cancer figure prominently. Your lucky number is 8.

Saturday, December 17 (Moon in Aries)   The accent is on a humanitarian project that will help many. Volunteer time and money to help those less fortunate than yourself. You'll meet an Aries who has pioneering ideas about the future—and wants to include you in a big project. Leave the past behind now.

Sunday, December 18 (Moon in Aries to Taurus 1:11 p.m.)   Your desire to make a dramatic new start could be curtailed by an associate who has other ideas. You may have to balance independence with cooperation in a partnership situation. Use charisma and charm to win your way in diplomatic manner. Your lucky number is 1.

Monday, December 19 (Moon in Taurus)   Keep a low profile; be patient! Impatience now at decision of associate is not advised. You'll need the company of others, particularly familiar faces from the past. Accept the love and affection offered by an older woman.

Tuesday, December 20 (Moon in Taurus to Gemini 4:43 p.m.)   Your spirits lift, energy surges upward and a partner who was reluctant becomes much more attentive. You'll attract generosity; a very special gift may be on the agenda. Someone you meet at a social event has a delightful tale to tell you. Your lucky number is 3.

Wednesday, December 21 (Moon in Gemini)   Calculate recent expenditures. See where you stand financially. You can get much detail work accomplished today. Just discipline yourself to review and to revise. You'll be able to correct past errors and gain a great feeling of satisfaction at a job well done.

Thursday, December 22 (Moon in Gemini to Cancer 9:35 p.m.) A romantic date turns out to be much more intense than expected. There's much to talk about, including deep inner feelings that have been long held back. Your personal views could undergo a dramatic change through this intimate sharing. The lucky number is 5.

Friday, December 23 (Moon in Cancer) Message from family member at a distance adds to the delight of the holiday season. You'll be reminded of long-ago times, putting you in a nostalgic mood. Treat yourself and loved ones to little luxuries and delicious food. Libra plays a major role.

Saturday, December 24 (Moon in Cancer) A mood of unreality surrounds your thoughts and feelings. You'll be moving in a dream world, more aware of imagination and fancy than of everyday matters. Religious or spiritual rites are favored. Let someone else handle the practical details. Your lucky number is 7.

Sunday, December 25 (Moon in Cancer to Leo 4:57 a.m.) Much could be required of you today, but you'll be able to deliver in a way that inspires confidence in others. Special commitment to one you love could be on the agenda, reaffirming the ties that bind. A prestigious person will be entertained in your home.

Monday, December 26 (Moon in Leo) Complete projects that have been delayed by holiday season. This is an excellent time to look at the big picture and reassess where you are heading. You'll tune into universal values, releasing petty fears or doubts. Aries plays a key role. Your lucky number is 9.

Tuesday, December 27 (Moon in Leo to Virgo 3:27 p.m.) New friends pop onto the scene. Be ready for a change of scenery and lively repartee. New modes of entertainment could be fun and exciting, especially if they bring you in touch with someone who helps transform a dream into reality. Leo plays a key role.

Wednesday, December 28 (Moon in Leo to Virgo 3:27 p.m.) Someone who figured prominently in your past returns. You'll have much to discuss, including where you've been and where you're going. Save time for family, a quiet social get-together and a special accent on home, food and cooking. The lucky number is 2.

Thursday, December 29 (Moon in Virgo) Take an optimistic look at the future. You'll have plenty of company wherever you go—your bright, cheerful attitude will draw people to you. A special message from someone at a distance thrills you—a fond dream is about to come true. Gemini is on the scene.

Friday, December 30 (Moon in Virgo to Libra 4:09 a.m.) You'll be drawn to quiet, routine, behind-the-scenes types of activities. A detail-minded mood helps you make lists of things to do, including resolutions for the new year. Come to terms also with hidden fears and doubts; erase them from the picture. The lucky number is 4.

Saturday, December 31 (Moon in Libra) The choice is yours between introvertish tendencies and a desire for change, variety and adventure. You'll probably be attracted to a select group of those who understand you—and want to share a special celebration. Virgo and Gemini figure prominently.

About This Series

This is one of a series of
twelve Day-by-Day Astrological Guides
for the signs in 1988
by Sydney Omarr

About the Author

Born on August 5, 1926, in Philadelphia, Sydney Omarr
was the only astrologer ever given full-time duty in the
U.S. Army as an astrologer. He also is regarded as the
most erudite astrologer of our time and the best-known,
through his syndicated column (300 newspapers) and
his radio and television programs (he is Merv Griffin's
"resident astrologer"). Omarr has been called the most
"knowledgeable astrologer since Evangeline Adams."
His forecasts of Nixon's downfall, the end of World
War II in mid-August of 1945, the assassination of
John F. Kennedy, Roosevelt's election to a fourth term
and his death in office ... these and many others
are on record and quoted enough to be considered
"legendary."